Self-Help and the Bible
Volumes 1 & 2

Tracy Harger

BALBOA.
PRESS
A DIVISION OF HAY HOUSE

Balboa Press books may be ordered through booksellers or by contacting:

Balboa Press
A Division of Hay House
1663 Liberty Drive
Bloomington, IN 47403
www.balboapress.com
1-(877) 407-4847

ISBN: 978-1-4525-4316-1 (sc)
ISBN: 978-1-4525-4315-4 (e)

Printed in the United States of America

Balboa Press rev. date: 12/21/2011

Self-Help and the Bible
Volume 1

Contents

Preface

In the early spring of 2008 my parents were traveling on vacation in central Arkansas (something they rarely done), and while shopping in a health food store there, the store owner slipped a DVD titled "The Secret" into their grocery bag. That DVD sat and collected dust until late summer when I decided to check it out for the purpose to determine if it was trash or not. I was impressed. Despite not having much exposure to the so called "self-help" movement, most of the information was very familiar; the reason for this was my background.

My background is in theology and as a theologian I had always steered clear of topics frowned upon by the conservative religious community. Unfortunately subject's such as positive thinking and the law of attraction has been haphazardly thrown into the same pot as tarot cards and Ouija boards. I was amazed to find so much subject matter that was theological in nature in a secular self-help video presentation. "The

Secret" really brought back some memories of my early teenage years.

Sometime during the mid to late seventies I remember watching a television program or video presentation featuring an enthusiastic elderly gentleman by the name of Glenn Coon. He had been a lifelong pastor and evangelist. I have never seen such energy and happiness in any person before. I can remember him now: leaping into the air and at the same time punching his fist out in front of him and yelling "The joy of Jesus". Pastor Coon wrote a book entitled "The ABC's of Bible prayer". The A stood for **ASK**, the B stood for **Believe**, and the C stood for Claim or **Receive**. Does this sound familiar? If you have not watched the DVD presentation of "The Secret", or have been exposed to the subject of self improvement it would be helpful to acquaint yourself with the topic before reading the first few chapters.

This book presupposes the notion that you are familiar with the material contained in either the book or DVD entitled "The Secret". If you are not, I am sure you are still in for an experience that could change your life. For easy reading, I have tried to keep this book as concise as possible and it has been printed with a larger font point. I have also deitalicized some words in scripture and have also taken the liberty to bold certain words in the subject paragraph and in the scriptural verse quoted in the paragraph. Some of the scriptures being presented will seem repetitive, but this book is based on a seminar and every verse read in the seminar is also printed in the book. Some things are too important not to repeat. Although I prefer the New Century Version of the Bible, I use a wide variety of versions in my lectures and in my studies. Since the Bible was not written in English, any English version will fail to fully convey the concepts and ideas expressed in the original Greek and Hebrew. This is why I do not exclusively use one version of the Bible with the thought that God endorses one version more than another.

Also I do not limit the scope of this book to the material contained in "The Secret". The subject matter necessitates that other laws and principles discussed by Bob Procter and others on "The Secret" DVD, but not specifically mentioned on "The Secret" DVD be pointed out. These other laws and principles just so happen to be related to current interests in the theological community, but due to the controversial nature of it, you will not hear a word of it from any pulpit. The issues discussed in "The Secret" are topics we will deal with. Whether the religious community likes it or not, they will have to deal with these issues because these issues deal with the character and nature of God.

This book follows the format of comparing scripture and quotes from the 1937 version of Think and Grow Rich by Napoleon Hill to popular self-help topics After reading several so called self-help books it becomes readily apparent that one can find more practical Christianity in literature advocating an optimistic and positive lifestyle than in living a life of a church going hypocrite that is negative and fault-finding most of the time. Self improvement books are beautiful in their own way. I refer frequently from some of these self-help books knowing that you may have already read them and feel more comfortable reading subject matter that is somewhat familiar. I am fully convinced that you will have more faith after reading this book. It is my deepest desire that you are inspired by this book and not offended. Keep in mind the subject matter you are about to read is similar to the ocean. The deeper they are, the more fun they are to explore.

Chapter One

Asking

Before we dive into the scriptures dealing with **asking** we need to perform a visualization exercise.

Imagine that you are the son or daughter of an extremely wealthy father. You are in your late teens or early twenties and live in a nice large house with a butler, a maid, and several brothers and sisters. Your father is the most faultfinding, negative person you have ever met. He keeps everybody in check by fear, and nobody wants to be around him. The problem is that your car is very old and is in such poor condition that getting a new car is the only option you have. You must confront your father about this situation. Reluctantly you make your way to the library where he is working. You stare at the ten foot tall mahogany doors that lead into the library, and then at the butler as he motions to you that he wants no part of this. The butler then turns to the maid and together they both run as if their lives were in danger. Feeling that you have no choice, you open the doors a little and with great trepidation approach the large teak wood and cherry inlaid mahogany desk. The dark stain of the desk matches the constant mood of your father. Your father gives you a look that says "You had better not even think of asking me for money or anything else" We will call this father "Father number one"

Now let us imagine the same thing only your father is the nicest, most generous, caring person you have ever met. He goes above and beyond all means to make sure that you are perfectly content and have need of nothing. The problem is your car. Your car (all eight of them) is new, but your father runs out to inform you that next years model has just came on the market and he wants to buy it for you. In fact he is begging you to let him buy you the newest model car he can find. What will you do? Will you receive what is rightfully yours as a child of such a wealthy parent? When you need some extra spending money to buy clothes or books for school, how do you approach your father? The doors going into his library are always open. The reason for this is that your father sits in his chair fantasizing about you running into the room and asking for money, help or anything else you could ever want. What does he want? He wants to spend every waking moment of his time with you-the apple of his eye! He sits behind his large teak wood and cherry inlaid mahogany desk looking out the window waiting for you to come, and ask for anything you may want. You are on his mind every waking moment. We will call this person "Father number two". When you pray to god, do you imagine him to be like father number one or father number two? We will refer to this analogy later. With that said let us read what the Bible says about asking.

Matthew 7:7-12 NKJV

[7] "**Ask**. And it will be given to you; seek, and you will find; knock, and it will be opened to you.[8] for everyone who **asks receives**, and he who seeks finds, and to him who knocks it will be opened. [9] Or what man is there among you who, if his son **asks** for bread, will give him a stone? [10] Or if he **asks** for a fish, will give him a serpent? 11 If you then, being evil, know how to give good gifts to your children, how much more will your father who is in heaven give good things to those who **ask** him![12] Therefore, whatsoever you want men to do to you, do also to them, for this is the law and the prophets."

John 14:14 NCV

"If you **ask** me for anything in my name, I will do it."

Ephesians 3:20 NIV

"Now to him who is able to do immeasurably more than all we **ask** or imagine, according to his power that is at work within us,"

There are three lines below that represent what Ephesians 3:20 is trying to say. The first line represents all we could possibly ask. The second line represents all we could imagine. I made this line longer because the mind can expand and think faster than thoughts can be vocalized. The third line represents the unlimited resources available to us.

Faith is another factor that we need to consider. "..according to his power that is at work within us," this may be referring to a person's faith when asking. Dr. Norman Vincent Peale wrote about this very subject by saying basically that our faith determines our blessings. (1)

Matthew 21:22 NKJV

"And whatsoever things you **ask** in prayer, **believing**, you will **receive**."

Notice how all three elements mentioned in The Secret video are present in this one verse and mentioned in context, and in the same manner the words are used in the video.

James 4:1-3 NIV

"What causes fights and quarrels among you? Don't they come from your desires that battle within you? [2] You want something but you don't get it. You kill and covet, but you cannot have what you want. You quarrel and fight. You do not have, because you do not **ask** God. [3]When you **ask**, you do not **receive**, because you **ask** with wrong motives, that you may spend what you get on your pleasures."

Notice that instead of arguing, fighting, killing, and coveting, we are to simply ask God. As long as we are not asking for something that is expressly forbidden for us to have or something outside of God's plan for us, we can expect a positive answer to our prayers. If I covet my neighbor's wife and plan to kill my neighbor to take his wife, do I have any business asking God in prayer to bless or condone my thoughts and actions?

1 John 5:14-15 NCV

"And this is the **boldness** that we have in God's presence: that if we **ask** God for anything that agrees with what he wants, he hears us.[15] If we know he hears us every time we **ask** him, we know we have what we **ask** from him."

In this verse there are three points of interest. First is the boldness that we have in God's presence is actually the level of comfort, or at easiness in his presence. This is why the analogy of father number two is given. We have to have a picture in our minds that we are speaking to someone in a relaxed and comfortable setting. We need to believe that God is working for us, not against us. Hebrews 4:16, is another one: "Let us come boldly to the throne of grace....." See also Hebrews 10:19. Just imagine that God is as generous and kind as father number two and you will be closer to living your life of abundance that God meant for you to live.

Second is the recognition of certain buzz words in the Bible. Sometimes the word "**if**", if used in a certain way, expresses doubt. Since a state of doubt is antagonistic to a state of faith, the word "**if**" is to be looked at as a negative word. On the other hand, the word "**know**" is a faith word. We will put know on our list of positive words. Notice the concrete faith of Paul found in Second Timothy 1:12 (NASB) ".....for I

know whom I have believed......." We will investigate some more buzz words later.

Third is the fact that we have to believe that God hears us when we ask him for anything. Read verse 15 out loud to yourself in the first person omitting the word if. Say something like "I know he hears me every time I ask him. I also know I have what I ask for from him because I know he hears me! This statement is full of faith. Notice how many times the buzz word "know" is used in that statement.

Most of the verses you have just read are actually promises. Promises have legal authority in universal court. When God says he will do something, the whole universe is watching to observe the outcome. Numbers 23:19 in the Contemporary English Version says that "God is no mere human! He doesn't tell lies or change his mind. God always keeps his promises." See also the New King James Version. The Bible is not just a manual on right living; it is a legal document of the highest authority.

Chapter Two

Believing

Believing (or faith) is the most common necessity mentioned in the Bible in connection with either working miracles or personal achievement. Anytime an unsuccessful attempt occurred in scripture at performing a miracle, lack of faith was given as the cause. The number of miracles Jesus performed is remarkable considering his ministry only lasted three and one half years. At the close of his gospel, the apostle John commented that if all of the works of Jesus were to be recorded, the world would not be large enough to contain such a volume of literature. As to the magnitude of supernatural phenomenon Jesus performed, Jesus himself predicted that someday we would perform far greater miracles than he did! We need to understand that the great men and women of the Bible did not do miracles because they were chosen to do so. They worked miracles because they had developed the faith to do so.

John 14:12-13 NCV

"I tell you the truth, whoever **believes** in me will do the same things that I do. Those who **believe** will do even greater things than these, because I am going to the father. 13 And if you **ask** for anything in my name, I will do it for you so that the father's glory will be shown through the Son."

Mark 11:24 NCV

"So I tell you to **believe** that you have **received** the things you **ask** for in prayer, and God will give them to you."

Believing that you have received something before you have actually received it fully in a physical sense is a little like an IOU. Think of it this way: an IOU from God is more solid than concrete. Take for example the story of the ten lepers. In Luke chapter 17:11-19 the story starts off with ten lepers keeping their distance between themselves and Jesus. They implored Jesus. "…have mercy on us." Jesus just looked at them and said "Go show yourselves to the priests". Everybody knows that lepers do not ask to be inspected by a priest unless they believe they have been completely cured of the disease. The lepers had so much faith in what Jesus had said that they immediately ran to the priests. There was no need to check to see if they had been healed or not. There was no question in their mind that if Jesus said so, it was a done deal. Verse 14 states that "…as they went, they were cleansed." Notice the word "**as**". That is another one of those buzz words. It is important for us to understand how this word is being used. Another example is found in Joshua chapter 3. The children of Israel was about to go in and posses the promised land. Only one thing stood in their way, the Jordan River. The instruction from God was that the bearers of the Ark of the Covenant were to march out into the river. This took faith. The mercy seat on the ark was made of pure gold, so it was no easy task to transport something that heavy. Now picture this. If you and everyone you know of lived in the desert all your lives then no one would know how to swim. Now just imagine your job is to be the first one in line to carry the ark into the river! How do you do it? No problem, God said he would take care of their (our) problems before they would adversely affect them (us). Verses 15 and 16 says that **as** soon as their feet touched the water, the river downstream of them flowed downstream, the river upstream of them flowed upstream, and they stepped out onto dry land. When God makes a way out of a difficult situation (an answer to prayer), does it seem like that way always involves faith on our part? All of this talk about having received something before you receive it sounds kind of strange, but Napoleon Hill put it this way:

"By following the instructions laid down in the chapters on autosuggestion, and the subconscious mind, as summarized in the chapter on autosuggestion, you may CONVINCE the subconscious mind that you *believe* you will receive that for which you ask, and it will act upon that belief, which your subconscious mind passes back to you in the form of "FAITH," followed by definite plans for procuring that which you desire." (2)

Mark 9: 20-24 NCV

"So the followers brought him to Jesus. As soon as the evil spirit saw Jesus, it made the boy lose control of himself, and he fell down and rolled on the ground, foaming at the mouth.

21 Jesus asked the boys father, "How long has this been happening?" The father answered, "Since he was very young. 22 The spirit often throws him into a fire or into water to kill him. **If** you can do anything for him, please have pity on us and help us."

23 Jesus said to the father, "you said, '**if** you can!' All things are possible for the one who believes."

24 Immediately the father cried out, "I do **believe**! Help me to **believe** more."

I have divided this story into several parts because there is much to learn from each part. Notice the word "**if**" and how it is used. You never want to say "if you can" to God. God wants to hear you say phrases like "I know you can." And "I know you hear me." In verse 23 is found one of the most important promises to mankind. Fans of any self improvement philosophy should make themselves familiar with it. Jesus makes the simple statement: "**All things are possible for the one who believes**." Is it possible that ten-thousand years from now we will finally realize that all things really were possible for us now, but we just lacked the necessary faith as a catalyst to take advantage of what was set before us? Imagine the universe at our fingertips, and we pass it up because we thought it was too good to be true. What if we actually lived in a world where truth was stranger and more wondrous than fiction, and the most valuable treasures in the universe were free? Here is another fitting statement from Mr. Hill.

"It is my duty, and a privilege to say I believe, and not without reason, that nothing is impossible to the person who backs DESIRE with enduring FAITH."(3)

Matthew 17:19-21 NKJV

"Then the disciples came to Jesus privately and said, "Why could we not cast it out?" 20 So Jesus said to them, "because of your unbelief; for assuredly, I say to you, if you have **faith** as a mustard seed, you will say to this mountain, 'Move from here to there,' and it will move; and nothing will be impossible for you. 21 However, this kind does not go out except by prayer and fasting."

From this statement we read that the disciples experienced failure because of unbelief. Also note prayer and fasting is mentioned as a perquisite to performing miracles of any kind. Before Jesus performed any miracles he fasted and prayed for six weeks! I doubt that he expects us to fast for such a long period of time, but a lifestyle of fasting and prayer is priceless. I do have friends and acquaintances that have performed miracles, and fasting has been a lifelong habit of theirs. I will not take time to explain the science of fasting here, but the internet can be informative on the subject, or just ask me if you happen to see me in a seminar.

Luke 9: 40-41 NCV

"I begged your followers to force the evil spirit out, but they could not do it." 41 Jesus answered, "You people have no **faith**, and your lives are all wrong. How long must I put up with you? Bring your son here."

God is patient, but here we see that our lack of faith tries his patients. Faithlessness on our part causes him great discomfort and frustration. The New Testament says that "...without faith it is impossible to please God, because anyone who comes to him must **believe** that he exist and that he rewards those who earnestly seek him." (4) Earnestly seeking God is another step mentioned several times in the Bible. When discussing the issue of seeking God, most Christians refer to Matthew 6:33-"But seek first the kingdom of God and his righteous, and all the things shall be added to you." NKJV There are many scripture references that discuss this topic, and we will look at some of these later on the chapter of prosperity.

Not only is it necessary to have faith in the existence of God, but we have to believe that God is the type of person who wants to reward us. Every verse in the Bible that describes God or the character of God, gives a description of our father number two. How would you feel if you were God and people treated you and talked to you as if you were father number one?

James 1:5-7 NIV

"If any of you lacks wisdom, he should **ask** God, who gives generously to all without finding fault, and it will be given to him. 6But when he **asks**, he must **believe** and not doubt, because he who doubts is like a wave of the sea, blown and tossed by the wind. 7That man should not think he will **receive** anything from the lord."

Compare this statement to one made by Mr. Hill:

"If you pray for a thing, but have fear as you pray that you may not receive it, or that your prayer may not be acted upon by Infinite Intelligence, your prayer will have been in vain."(5)

Matthew 21:21 NKJV

"So Jesus answered and said to them, "Assuredly, I say to you, if you have **faith** and do not doubt, you will not only do what was done to the fig tree, but also if you say to this mountain, 'Be removed and be cast into the sea,' it will be done."

Let's see if what Mr. Hill has to say about having faith:

"FAITH is the basis of all "miracles," and all mysteries which cannot be analyzed by the rules of science!"(6)

"It is a well known fact one comes, finally, to BELIEVE whatever one repeats to one's self, *whether the statement be true or false.* If a man repeats a lie over and over, he will eventually accept the lie as truth. Moreover, he will BELIEVE it to be truth. Every man is what he is because of the DOMINATING THOUGHTS which he permits to occupy his mind."(7)

"Here is a most significant fact – the subconscious mind takes any orders given to it in a spirit of absolute FAITH, and acts upon those orders, although the orders often have to be presented *over and over again*, through repetition, before they are interpreted by the subconscious mind."(8)

Notice the element of repetition in the last two quotes. Are we not told in 1 Thessalonians 5:17 to "Pray without ceasing"? Remember this when you read the chapter on persistence. Notice also that Napoleon says that the dominating thoughts that we permit to occupy our minds makes us what we are. The Bible says something very similar. "Be careful what you think, because your thoughts run your life."(9) The story of the raising of Lazarus found in the eleventh chapter of John has other important elements that we need to acknowledge. Notice verse 4 and verses 17-44. I will be quoting excerpts from the New International Version. Please read the entire story in your Bible.

Jesus was less than two miles from Jerusalem when Lazarus was taken deathly ill and messengers dispatched to Bethany where Jesus was. The messengers expected Jesus, upon hearing of Lazarus's condition, to rush back to Jerusalem to heal Lazarus. Instead Jesus seemed not at all interested in doing what they thought to be the most direct and logical action in this crisis situation. Jesus said "This sickness will not end in death" and it did (from our point of view). So maybe what we call death, He calls sleep. See verses eleven and twelve. What Jesus calls death is referred to as the second death. See Revelation 2:11, 20:7-10. One death we are to dread and not the other, but most people dread the other and not the one. The reason given for not healing Lazarus was for "God's glory". In the minds of the people there was a difference between healing a person and resurrecting a person. Jesus was trying to dispel this false notion and demonstrate to them that it was no more difficult for the power of God to bring someone back to life than it was to heal a minor injury. We need to learn from this. It is no more difficult for God to give us great things than it is small things. The only difference is in our minds.

Jesus waits four days and then makes his way back to Jerusalem. Martha meets Jesus in the outskirts of the city and reminds him that if he had the sense to obey the admonishment of the messengers, this crisis would have been adverted. Then in verse twenty two she gives the only real statement of faith found in this story. She says "I know that even now God will give you whatever you ask." This statement seems a little out of place; it seems to be written more for our benefit in our time than to be a natural part of the conversation in their time. After Jesus states his nature, he asks Martha "Do you believe this? I believe Jesus was trying to get her to say "yes, I believe" in response. There is a lot of discussion in the self-help movement about the power of words, or the power of the spoken word. If Jesus wanted Martha to say "Yes, I believe" then he would also want us to say the same also. After Martha left, it was Mary's turn to remind Jesus that if he had followed the plans that the household had initially agreed to that he should have done, this crisis would have been adverted. How many times have we thought that if God was as smart as us and that if he would have followed plan A, like we agreed with ourselves that he should have done in the first place, then this crisis in our lives might have been avoided. Wouldn't it be easier to just have faith?

When Jesus approached the tomb and asked that the tomb be opened, Martha intervened because of the advanced state of decomposition of her brother. If she had any idea of what Jesus was about to do, she wouldn't have said a word. And this was after Jesus had told her that he was the "resurrection and the life"! Is it possible that Jesus can plainly tell us the most valuable secrets and we don't understand what he is saying? Or we do not believe what he is saying? Jesus then said to Mary "Did I not tell you that if you believed, you would see the glory of God?" What Jesus says next is important because contextually the words are meant to be information that we need. This whole story seems to be a set up for Jesus to give us valuable information. Jesus looks up and says "Father, I thank you that you have heard me. I knew that you always hear me, but I said this for the benefit of the people..." What we have here is gratitude, total faith that God is going to hear him, total faith that God has already heard him, and the **I know** buzz words. What a winning combination. We need these elements in our lives. When I talk to God I have to have total faith that he has already heard me and that he continues to hear me. The gratitude that I have for God at that moment springs forth from the fact that **I know** that he is going to answer my prayer. People who are close to God are very sure that they have what they ask because they know the character of God is much more generous , kind , and forgiving than the analogy that we gave of father number two. They know this through the time they spend in quiet meditation in the presence of God. I sincerely believe that the heroes of the bible did not perform miracles because they were any more special or chosen than we are today. If we would develop our faith to the same degree that they did, we could do the same miracles that they did.

Luke 17:5-6 NCV

"The apostles said to the Lord, "Give us more **faith**!" 6 The lord said, "If your **faith** were the size of a mustard seed, you could say to this mulberry tree, 'Dig yourself up and plant yourself in the sea,' and it would obey you"

Romans 10:17 AMP

"So **faith** comes by hearing [what is told], and what is heard comes by the preaching [of the message that came from the lips] of Christ (the Messiah Himself).

The Amplified Bible makes it clear that hearing the words of Christ gives faith. I had this in mind when writing this book; that is why they are integrated into the first chapters of this book. If you are around people who talk doubt all the time and say things like "I don't believe it" then you will be affected by it. If, on the other hand, you associate with people of faith and you hear stories of how they achieved great things through visualization, positive thinking habits, and expectant faith; this will also have an affect on you. Some say this is what Hebrews 10:25 was referring to. People of faith would get together to discuss the weeks past events. The few who had the faith to work miracles inspired faith in those who did not have the faith to perform miracles. Over time as people heard more stories and witnessed miracles themselves, they in turn developed the faith to perform miracles. We are to exhort, encourage and inspire one another. As a general rule, one does not make it a habit to associate with negative thinkers and doubters if one wants to develop more faith. Faith, like doubt, is a lifestyle, a thinking process that is developed over time.

Habakkuk 2:4 NCV

"The evil nation is very proud of itself; it is not living as it should. But those who are right with God will live by **faith**."

Chapter three

Faith, Love, and Fear

Love		Fear
Faith		Doubt

As seen in the diagram, collectively love and faith is directly opposed to fear and doubt. I never really thought about it until I noticed this relationship kept coming up repeatedly in the Bible and in Think and Grow Rich. The relationship between love and faith seems to be just as symbiotic as fear and doubt. In ones life when a person moves toward faith and love, in effect they are moving away from fear and doubt, and vice versa. As I study the subject further it appears that fear of an individual is nullified by unconditional love for that individual. All of this is fitting for the first century during which Christians were being persecuted for their faith. An absence of fear would be necessary to carry out evangelistic endeavors that were punishable by torture, prison, or death. Most Christians are familiar with the Apostle Paul's analogy in Ephesians chapter six of putting on the whole armor of God. The shield of **faith** and the helmet of salvation are described in verses sixteen and seventeen. It is interesting to note that when giving the same analogy to the Thessalonians, Paul changed the words around. In 1 Thessalonians 5:8 he talks of putting on the breastplate of **faith and love**. The combination of faith and love, and the opposition of love and fear are repeatedly found in Paul's writings. Let's see what else Paul has to say about faith, love, and fear.

Galatians 5:6 NCV

When we are in Christ Jesus, it is not important if we are circumcised or not. The important thing is **faith**—the kind of **faith** that works through **love**.

2 Timothy 1:7 NKJV

For God has not given us the spirit of **fear**, but of power and of **love** and of a sound mind.

Note that Second Timothy was the last letter Paul wrote before getting his head chopped off; and here he is talking of power, love, and sound mind! Paul was a person that didn't let external circumstances influence his mood or his mind. Should we not do the same?

1 John 4: 17-18 NCV

"This is how **love** is made perfect in us: that we can be without **fear** on the day God judges us, because in this world we are like him. 18 where God's **love** is, there is no **fear**, because God's perfect **love** drives out **fear**. It is punishment that makes a person **fear**, so **love** is not made perfect in the person who **fears**."

Napoleon Hill divided love into two parts, love (spiritual) and sex (physical). So instead of describing two parts, he describes three. Notice how he describes the relationship of the three:

"The emotions of FAITH, LOVE, and SEX are the most powerful of all the major positive emotions. When the three are blended, they have the effect of "coloring" the vibration of thought in such a way that it instantly reaches the subconscious mind, where it is changed into its spiritual equivalent, the only form that induces a response from Infinite Intelligence.

Love and faith are psychic; related to the spiritual side of man. Sex is purely biological, and related only to the physical. The mixing, or blending, of these three emotions has the effect of opening a direct line of communication between the finite, thinking mind of man, and Infinite Intelligence."(10)

"It is a known fact that the emotion of LOVE is closely akin to the state of mind known as FAITH, and this for the reason that Love comes very near to translating one's thought impulses into their spiritual equivalent."(11)

Now we look into a darker aspect of this chapter. What happens if you separate love from faith? If you do this then you will have something that should be undesirable to us all.

1 Corinthians 13:2 NKJV

"And though I have the gift of prophecy, and understand all mysteries and all knowledge, and though I have all **faith**, so that I could remove mountains, but have not **love**, I am nothing."

The Bible is clear that performing miracles, no matter how wondrous and benevolent they may be, is not a sign that you are a good person or on God's side of the conflict. An example that most people are familiar with is the account of Jannes and Jambres who contended against Moses using magic. (See Exodus 7:11-12, and 2 Timothy 3:8) All parties involved had faith, but only one had love. The New Testament characterizes the wicked as those who perform miracles, cast out demons, and prophesy all in the name of God! (See Matthew 7:21-23) Whether a person is good or evil, faith is still a necessity to accomplish greatness. Jesus used faith to help people; Nimrod used faith to control people. Faith is the fuel that will propel you to the highest places in the universe, but you have to decide where that place is. Lucifer was once one of the most powerful, most beautiful beings in the universe, but he chose the negative path of darkness and disobedience. Every conscience moment of our lives we choose our destiny by our thoughts. The spiritual battle is largely a battle for the mind. Some people say we have a heaven to gain and a hell to shun. I say we need to produce and encourage positive thoughts and steer away from negative thoughts. I think this is what the apostle Paul meant when he said in Romans 12:2 to not be conformed to this world, but be transformed by the renewing of our minds, that we may prove what is good and acceptable, and perfect will of God. The last phrase of Romans 12:2 is a bit foggy. The New Century Version says that we will then be able to decide what God wants for us, and we will know what is good and pleasing to God. To me this is saying that a continual habit of positive thinking will bring clarity into my life. No more guessing what God's will is or if I am on the right path. Every day becomes an adventure of good, happy thoughts, and good works. We go through the day without worry, confident that whatever happens will work in our favor to bring us ultimate prosperity and happiness. (See Romans 8:28)

Chapter Four

The Seen and The Unseen

I had not planned to discuss quantum physics, but it is in the Bible and almost every book on the law of attraction and the mind deals with it. If we study the philosophies of the law of attraction and how they relate to quantum physics from books written by authors like Bob Procter and David Cameron Gikandi, and then compare this with what the Bible says what we find is nothing short of amazing. What most self-help gurus have been telling us for years, has been in the Bible all along. Despite this, you will probably never hear a sermon on it. There seems to be some unspoken rule in some conservative churches that you don't mix physics with theology. Let's start by looking at an equation that we are all familiar with.

E=MC²

Notice how the invisible side (E) is equal to the visible side (MC2). They are both the same, just different speeds. If you take any matter and propel it to the speed of ninety billion kilometers per second, it then becomes energy. For our purposes of learning we need to see the differences between energy and matter. Look at the image below and notice some of the buzz words included with energy and matter. Believing and faith could be placed on the energy side. With this in mind some Bible verses become very revealing.

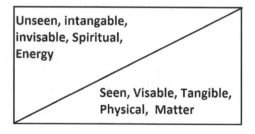

Discussing physics with theology is a little tricky. It's like a toymaker in a toyshop. The toymaker not only designs the toys, but plans the box the toys are going to stored in. The box is built first, and then the toys. The universe as we know it is like the toys. The box is length, breadth, height, time, all laws of the universe, and the various dimensions. This is where Jesus comes in to the story. In church we hear sermons about Jesus being our creator and all of that is fine. But we need to understand one thing, Jesus didn't just make the toys, he built the toy box!

Colossians 1:15-17 NCV

"No one can **see** God, but Jesus is exactly like him. He ranks higher than everything that has been made. 16 Through his power all things were made—things in heaven and on earth, things **seen** and **unseen**, all powers, authorities, lords, and rulers. All things were made through Christ and for Christ. 17 He was there before anything was made, and all things continue because of him."

Romans 1:20-21 NCV

"There are things about him that people **cannot see**— his eternal power and all the things that make him God. But since the beginning of the world those thing have been easy to understand by what God has made. So people have no excuse for the bad things they do. 21 They knew God, but they did not give glory to God or thank him. Their thinking became useless. Their foolish minds were filled with darkness."

Humans have no excuse, the character of God is written in every detail of his creation. The toys themselves proclaim the skill and craftsmanship of the toymaker. People need to stop worrying, and stop living life as if God was like father number one. Go to a botanical garden; get out in nature and see what God is like. Abundance and prosperity is God's middle name. He longs to give us the life of our dreams, the key to which may lie in something we have control over: our thoughts. Notice what Mr. Hill has to say about it.

"Moreover—and this is of stupendous importance—this earth, every one of the billions of individual cells of your body, and every atom of matter, *began as an intangible form of energy.* Desire is thought impulse! Thought impulses are forms of energy."(12)

We can daily transform ourselves into a better person by controlling our thoughts. It is the things not seen that control the things that are seen. In fact the scriptures mention that the origin of the universe was not from matter, but energy.

Hebrews 11:1-3 NIV

"Now faith is being sure of what we hope for and certain of what we **do not see**. 2 This is what the ancients were commended for. 3 By faith we understand that the universe was formed at God's command, so that what **is seen** was **not** made out of what was **visible**."

The Bible is quite clear; our focus is to be on the world of the unseen. Things were different when we were children. A child lives in a world of make believe surrounded by unlimited opportunities. When we were young we had no fear and every day was an adventure. Now fast forward to middle age or old age and millions of people are desperately trying to deprogram themselves of fear and worry. We scour pages and pages of self help books trying to regain our lost innocents. And then we read in the Bible that we must ultimately be like a child anyway, in that respect we come full circle. (See Luke 18:17)

2 Corinthians 4:18 NKJV

"While we do not look at the things which are **seen**, but at the things which are **not seen**. For the things which are **seen** are temporary, but the things which are **not seen** are eternal"

Some forms of energy are eternal. Forms of matter are transient in nature and form the basis of what many call the illusion of the conditions around us. I believe God created it this way for our enjoyment because we are spiritual beings inhabiting a physical body. The universe was created in such a way that allows its inhabitants to enjoy life to the fullest, even far beyond present human comprehension. But something went terribly wrong and beings who had known nothing but blissful happiness and joy beyond description found themselves suffering sadness and anxiety. The only obvious recourse a loving God has is to immediately begin a restoration process. This process begins with our thoughts. No matter where we have been or what our present condition is, right now we can change for the better.

2 Corinthians 5:7 NCV

"We live by what we believe, not by what we can see."

That last quote is my favorite. It concisely sums up what we read whole books to understand. This next quote clearly states that our conflicts are not with things that are seen, but unseen.

Ephesians 6:12 NKJV

"For we do not wrestle against flesh and blood, but against principalities, against powers, against the rulers the darkness of this age, against spiritual hosts of wickedness in the heavenly places."

Now let's look at the same verse in the Contemporary English Version.

"We are not fighting against humans. We are fighting against forces and authorities and against rulers of darkness and powers in the spiritual world."

Now let's look at the same verse in the New International Readers Version.

"Our fight is not against human beings. It is against the rulers, the authorities and the powers of this dark world. It is against the spiritual forces of evil in the heavenly world."

Any physical threat that I perceive is just a manifestation of spiritual forces, therefore any defense or counter attack will have to be of spiritual origin. The rest of Ephesians list the offensive and defensive elements necessary for spiritual warfare; notice that faith is listed along with the word of God as essential elements necessary to deal with spiritual forces. This is testament to the fact that the word of God has authority over all created beings in the universe.

Chapter Five

The Law of Attraction

The Bible has a little to say about the law of attraction. The main emphasis of scripture is on moral standing and not attracting a wealthy lifestyle. Nevertheless, the viewpoint of the Bible is that those who use the law of attraction favorably are wise and those who do not are fearful. We have just read in chapter three that where God's love is, there is no fear, and so we can assume that a person that has fear in their life has an absence of God's love in their life. This makes the story of Job even more interesting. Job uses the law of attraction to gain enormous wealth, and then fear creeps in to destroy it. I believe Job developed "what if syndrome". What if this happens, and what if that happens. These are words of doubt. Rock solid faith leaves no room for doubt and totally ignores fear. Still, Job was a good man. God was always number one in

Job's life; Job just momentarily lost his bearings and sailed into the sea of fear. We must take heart least the same thing happens to us and, like Job, we lose everything. The Bible shows us that the greatest people in history have their ups and downs. We can learn from their mistakes, let us learn from Job's.

Job 3:25 NCV

"Everything I feared and dreaded has happened to me."

Proverbs 10:24 NCV

"Evil people will get what they fear most, but good people will get what they want most."

Proverbs 11:27 NKJV

"He who earnestly seeks good finds favor, but trouble will come to him who seeks evil."

Is it a possibility that the wants (desires) and fears of our life make up our dominating thoughts? Hill seems to think so.

"...our brains become magnetized with the dominating thoughts which we hold in our minds, and, by means with which no man is familiar, these "magnets" attract to us the forces, the people, the circumstances of life which harmonize with the nature of our *dominating* thoughts."(13)

If a person's dominating thoughts determine their circumstances then we can look at a person's circumstances and understand their dominating thoughts. With this in mind let's look at the lives of Jesus and the apostles. Some critics point out the poverty stricken lifestyle that haunted Jesus and the apostles is a contradiction to the so called "prosperity gospel" or the law of attraction. When the facts are examined it is clearly seen that the opposite is true. The poverty of Jesus is simply a testament to the totally selfless character of God. It seems from his actions that the thoughts that consumed Jesus were those of helping others and training twelve young men to continue his work after his ascension. The apostles were to busy trying to build a church and spread the gospel to all the earth and they didn't have time to live a life of wealth and prosperity. In the minds of the apostles any thoughts of worldly prosperity and leisure must have seemed sinful seeing they believed that the world was going to end in their day. Any thoughts or actions that distracted the apostles from accomplishing their mission must have been looked at as immoral. All generations of people mentioned in the Bible thought the world was going to end in their day, and they acted accordingly. I will discuss this fact at length in another book that I am writing. As for the debate on prosperity, we will discuss that in another chapter.

Chapter Six

The Law of Polarity

I never really thought about the law of polarity until I read about it in self-help literature. It exists in theology, but without a name. The basic Christian theological construct of the universe contains what others may call the law of polarity, but until recently theologians didn't call it anything, we just thought that's the way the universe was made. At this point I must say that theology at the university level is somewhat different than at the local church level. In the university we discuss deep issues of thought that are never supposed to be discussed in church. Like it or not, church is a business and if you scare away the tithe paying members then the bills will not get paid. That is why so many churches put people to sleep with textbook sermons that we have all heard since childhood. I have nothing against church, but there are many fascinating subjects in scripture that are being ignored. I have adapted what you are about to read with more familiar terminology to make it easier to understand. The basic theological construct goes as follows:

In the beginning there was nothing but God; the being we call God the father. There was no space, no matter, no time, no height breath, or depth, no dark matter, no electrons, protons, or neutrons. Do you get the picture? Then God did something, the reason of which can be debated for years. He cloned himself. The second part was called God the son. Both parts are identical in character, thought, and motive, yet both equally God. Truly God the son was begotten and not created, for it is he who created everything in the universe. So God set out to create, and the first thing to be brought into existence was a toy box! That right, what we call matter, energy, and all the laws of the universe. Colors had to be created. You wouldn't know what white was without black and vise versa. The same with emotions, love cannot exist without hate, or happiness without sadness. God had to create equal amounts of all things good and evil in the universe. You cannot have righteousness without unrighteousness; there are always equal amounts of both in the universe. After creating all laws and things (no life yet), God took all things evil and unpleasant and locked it away in a room (that's what I'm calling it). Then God creates the various life forms in the universe. For eons the angels and other planetary inhabitants knew nothing but happiness and joy beyond our (or their) comprehension. Life was simple and abundant beyond description. There was only one rule: Don't go into the room where unrighteousness and evil existed. God could go into the room and come out unaffected, but no one else could. This may be where we get the metaphors of *Pandora's Box* or *Jennie in a bottle*. We are told that God is surrounded by light so bright the no one can dwell in his presence (1 Tim.6:15-17). Only a few inhabitants of the universe have been granted the privilege of serving in the presence of God the father and Lucifer was one of those few. Some theologians believe that before his fall, Lucifer was the most powerful and the most beautiful created being in the universe. Lucifer was told that only God could know good and evil. At some point of time Lucifer coveted the title and position of God, and so took it upon himself to go into the room and acquaint himself with what was forbidden. In doing so he committed the first sin for sin is the transgression of the law (1John

3:4). Ever since that time he has been spreading the lie that the entire universe should have the freedom to know good and evil and act on it as he has done. Such thinking disregards the consequences of disobedience, and replaces faith in God with distrust. Did Lucifer not tell Eve that she would be like God, knowing good and evil (Gen. 3:5)? God never meant for anyone to know evil. This is what restoration is all about; it is about God putting the Jennie back into the bottle. I am OK with the theories of equal amounts of good and evil in the universe, but I also know that one day all evil will be once again locked up in a room. This time we won't have a key, and that is alright with me.

Chapter Seven

Prosperity

Years ago I went to a job interview with a Christian themed company and as the interview progressed the human resource manager asked me my opinion of Joel Osteen. I honestly replied that I thought that Joel was a positive person with a positive message. I was then informed by the human resource manager that we were saved through church doctrine and not through anything relating to positive thinking. Needless to say I did not get the job. Before I was allowed to leave the interview I had to sit through a short lecture on the hazards of the so called "prosperity gospel". This wasn't the first time I been warned of the dangers of believing in the so called false doctrine of prosperity.

I was raised up in a very conservative Christian environment and have been exposed to sights and experiences that I don't talk about much because they are just too unbelievable. I'm not going to get into details about elderly people pinching themselves with pliers, or adolescents having their genitals removed for spiritual reasons, but there is a section of society that pushes the limits of the religious right. Sad to say, a part of this movement is the belief that the road to heaven always runs through the valley of extreme poverty. I have seen good, well meaning Christians turn down opportunities to make money and get ahead in life because they were taught that it took only a small amount of money to send them to hell. They equate money with eternal damnation and poverty with heaven. This view of theirs reflects upon the character of God. What God is this that delights in seeing his children suffer in poverty? What is the point in going to heaven if we will have to spend an eternity in poverty? The Bible is very plain about the character of God, The habit of ignoring the parts of the Bible that conflict with long held beliefs can lead us down a dark path. Because I have seen people spend their entire lives in extreme poverty and pain due to their religion, I write this chapter. Remember the analogy of father number one and father number two as you read these verses.

John 10:10 AMP

"The thief comes only in order to steal and kill and destroy. I came that they have and **enjoy life**, and have it in **abundance** (to the full, till it overflows)"

James 1:17 AMP

"Every **good gift** and every perfect (free, large, full) gift is from above; it comes down from the father of all [that gives] light, in [the shining of] Whom there can be no variation [rising or sitting] or shadow cast by His turning [as in a eclipse]."

Psalm 84:11 NKJV

"For the Lord God is a sun and shield; the Lord will **give grace** and glory; no **good thing** will he withhold from those who walk uprightly."

I also like to read this verse in the Contemporary English Version where the last part says that God treats us with kindness and with honor, never denying any good thing to those who live right. These next two verses combine courage, obedience to God's law, and prosperity. Apparently if we have the first two then the third won't be far behind.

1 Chronicles 22:12-13 AMP

"Only may the lord give you wisdom and understanding as you are put in charge of Israel, that you may **keep the law of the lord** your God. 13 Then you will **prosper** if you are careful to keep and fulfill the statutes and ordinances with which the Lord charged Moses concerning Israel. **Be strong** and of good courage. Dread not and **fear not**; be not dismayed."

Joshua 1:7-8 AMP

"Only you **be strong** and very courageous, that you may do according to the law which Moses My servant commanded you. Turn not from it to the right hand or to the left, that you may prosper wherever you may go. 8 This **Book of the Law** shall not depart from your mouth, but you shall meditate in it day and night, that you may observe and do according to all that is written in it. For then you shall make your way **prosperous**, and then you shall deal wisely and have good **success**."

Proverbs 28:25 NIV

"A greedy man stirs up dissention, but he who **trusts in the Lord** will **prosper**."

3 John: 2 NKJV

"Beloved, I pray that you may **prosper** in all things and be **in health**, just as your **soul prospers**."

Philippians 4:19 NCV

"My God will use his wonderful **riches** in Christ Jesus **to give** you everything you need."

Romans 8:32 NIrV

"God did not spare his own son. He gave him up for us all. Then won't he also **freely give us everything else**?"

Does this verse not speak to the generosity of God? We have just read verse after verse about God wanting to give us something. Where did Bible believers ever get the idea that God wanted us to live in poverty? This next verse reminds me of Joel Osteen. It doesn't matter how many times he quotes it, I will never tire of hearing it. This is God talking to the Jews living in Babylon (Iraq). Imagine being kidnapped and taken by force to a foreign country where you don't speak their language and financially have to start over again. Any normal person would feel like giving up. Fortunately we serve a God that sends messages through his prophets to not give up. He says things like "build houses, plant gardens, get married and have children", and if the weather is not too hot outside, play badminton! In other words: even though your world may have been turned up-side down, **live life**. God does not want us to sit around and feel sorry for ourselves all the time. Knowing the story around this one verse will help put it in context. Please read the entire twenty ninth chapter.

Jeremiah 29:11 NIV

"For I know the plans I have for you," declares the LORD, "plans to **prosper** you and not to harm you, plans to **give you hope** and a future."

I believe humans have little comprehension of what prosperity is. We have just not experienced it. Some multimillionaires commit suicide because of stress while others living in poverty are happy and content. Is prosperity a frame of mind which cannot be seen or measured, or is it a combination of many things which are controlled by the thoughts we think and the decisions we make? Is it possible that the prosperity mankind has experienced over the last six thousand years is infinitesimal compared to what God has planned for us in eternity. If so then our basis for gauging prosperity is inadequate. Whatever definition we may have for prosperity, if it is ego centered, it is probably not the kind of prosperity God wants us to have.

Chapter Eight

Persistence & Forgiveness

I grouped persistence and forgiveness together for the reason of the answer Jesus gave when his followers asked him how to pray. The followers of Jesus noticed that the followers of John the Baptist were being taught to pray a certain way. Feeling that they were missing out on something, they came to Jesus and said something like "teach us to pray like they do". Jesus then gave them a two part answer found in Luke chapter eleven. The first part contained forgiveness and the second part contained persistence. The first part of the answer simply contained five elements. Jesus said that when praying to the father we are to say:

1. May your name be kept holy.
2. May your kingdom come.

3. Give us the food we need each day.

4. Forgive us our sins.

5. Do not cause us to be tempted.

In verse four, where it talks about forgiveness, a reason is given for the forgiveness. Verse four says to forgive us our sins because we forgive everyone who has ever done us wrong. We cannot have one without the other. This is made clear in Matthew's version of the story (see Matt. 6:14-15). Matthew also is the only gospel writer that tells the parable of the unforgiving servant (see Matt. 18: 21-35). The fact is that people will not get to heaven without a spirit of forgiveness toward others; this parable makes that clear.

Colossians 3:12-13 NASB

"So, as those who have been chosen of God, holy and beloved, put on a heart of compassion, kindness, humility, gentleness and patience; [13]bearing with one another, and **forgiving** each other, whoever has a complaint against anyone; just as the Lord **forgave** you, so also should you."

The timelessness of faith and forgiveness

This topic still sparks controversy among some theologians. The general consensus use to be that

God alone is timeless, but as we become more open-minded, we see the universe and our relationship to it in a different light. The timelessness of forgiveness is simply a concept. It is an easy task to forgive someone who has wronged us in the past; we have a clear record of the event. But suppose we expand our awareness and forgiveness up in all directions and into the future. Let's call this eternal forgiveness. We accept the fact that even though we have not been offended yet, the person or persons offending us has already been forgiven for the act. This way there is no longer any need for anyone to ask for our forgiveness because they have already been forgiven. Keep this in mind when you meet new people. Every person we meet is a potential best friend for eternity. It is important that we express kindness and compassion to all we meet in life. We may even meet someone that is severely retarded or deformed, but in heaven they will be restored and will remember our kindness.

The timelessness of faith is also a fascinating concept. Bible scholars have always assumed that for a miracle to be preformed, someone had to have faith. Also when someone failed to perform a miracle, lack of faith was the problem. There is nothing wrong with these assumptions for there is a considerable amount of scripture to support them. Here is the enigma. There is a story in the Bible about a funereal procession in the desert (2 Kings 13:20-21). It was in the spring of the year and as they were traveling to the burial plot, they saw a band of Moabite raiders. They hid themselves as best as they could, but had to lower the corpse of their friend into a hole in the ground due to lack of space. As the corpse touched the bottom of the hole, the dead man came to life! Who had faith? The intention was not to bury the man in the hole to begin with. At that time the goal of the funeral procession was to hide, not bring their friend back to life. This resurrection was totally unexpected. The truth is that Elisha was buried in that hole, and when the corpse touched Elisha's bones the dead man came to life. I believe that it was the faith of Elisha that brought that man to life. How can a dead man's faith work a miracle? Elisha apparently expanded has awareness of thought through time and with that he also expanded his faith through time also. How much faith did Elisha have? We get a clue from is conversation with Elijah (2 Kings 2:9-11). Elisha said to Elijah that whatever faith Elijah had, he wanted twice that amount; and he got it! We have to consider the nature of faith may be much larger than what we have imagined. Faith, like other attributes in self improvement, is free and can be developed.

Now back to what Jesus said about persistence. We have to consider the source. Luke was a medical doctor, one of the few apostles that had any formal education at all. His conversation was more thorough and he had an eye for detail. For example, when comparing the same events of Matthew 24 to Luke 21 we find that Luke talks of fearful sights and great signs in the heavens; a detail not mentioned in the gospel of Matthew. Considering the fact that Luke was more educated and probably more intelligent than most of the other apostles, why is it that the two main parables on persistence are found only in the gospel of Luke? Was Luke the only person to recognize the importance of this attribute? See for yourself. Read these thoroughly.

Luke 11:5-10 NCV

"Then Jesus said to them, "Suppose one of you went to your friend's house at midnight and said to him, 'Friend, loan me three loaves of bread. 6 A friend of mine has come into town to visit me, but I have nothing for him to eat.' 7 Your friend inside the house answers, 'Don't bother me! The door is already locked, and my children and I are in bed. I cannot get up and give you anything.' 8 I tell you, if friendship is not enough to make him get up to give you the bread, your **boldness** will make him get up and give you whatever you need. 9 So I tell you, ask, and God will give to you. Search, and you will find. Knock, and the door will open for you. 10 Yes, everyone who asks will receive. The one who searches will find. And everyone who knocks will have the door opened."

Notice the word boldness in verse eight. We have discussed that word before. The context that the word boldness is used is synonymous with the word persistence. Boldness is an attitude.

Luke 18:1-8 NKJV

"Then He spoke a parable to them, that men always ought to pray and not lose heart, 2 saying: "There was in a certain city a judge who did not fear God nor regard man. 3 Now there was a widow in that city; and she came to him, saying, 'Get justice for me from my adversary.' 4 And he would not for a while; but afterward he said within himself, 'Though I do not fear God nor regard man, 5 yet because this widow troubles me I will avenge her, lest by her continual coming she weary me.'" 6 Then the Lord said, "Hear what the unjust judge said. 7 And shall God not avenge His own elect who cry out day and night to Him, though He bears long with them? 8 I tell you that He will avenge them speedily. Nevertheless, when the Son of Man comes, will He really find faith on the earth?"

Now back to our analogy of father number two. These two parables take that another step further. Remember that father number two eagerly looked out the window looking for his daughter to come to visit him, and he always had his door open. Imagine now that he sends a message to his daughter with two instructions:

Number 1. No matter what the butler, or the maid or the gardener or anyone else tells you, come see me every day.

Number 2. If by chance you come to see me and the door is locked, be **bold**, start knocking and **do not stop knocking until I open the door.**

There are hundreds of verses of scripture about the character and nature of God that if applied to the analogy of father number two will give us an accurate portrayal of God in our minds. This will help us visualize God more accurately when we communicate with him. God wants us to grab a hold of him and not let go. Late one night Jacob was trying to get some sleep and God grabbed Jacob in such a way as to make him think he was being attacked (see Gen. 32:24-30). The end result of Jacob's struggle with God was that he was blessed by God. This makes me think, what does God have to do to us to get us to spend time with him?

Chapter Nine

The Nature of God and Man

It stands to reason that all of our asking, believing and hope of receiving depends on our perception of God. If I am asking somebody of something, and I honestly believe that they are not the kind of person that would give anything good to anybody, then do I have a reason to expect anything from them? How does this attitude affect your faith that this person will give you anything at all? I believe that most modern religions have got the cart before the horse so to speak. Before any church or denomination should ask anyone to ask, believe, or expect to receive anything from God, they need to explain what kind of person God is. This is true especially for little children. Imagine having gone through an extremely abusive childhood which was filled with negative paradigms of God, and then you decide to try out religion only to find the results disappointing. If a stranger calls me up, I want to know about this person before I spend a lot of time on the phone with them. The same is true with God. The truth is that we can spend a lifetime in church and never hear a sermon on the extreme generous nature of God. When I try to explain this to some people they do not believe me because is goes against all they believe about God and religion. Does anyone read the Bible for themselves anymore? The generous nature of God is something we need to understand because this answers the question why. Why should I expect what I ask for, when I ask for it? The truth is that God is such a generous; giving person that he gives people what they ask for even when it is the wrong thing! Even when he does not want to give us what we ask for, he gives it to us anyway! If you combine these facts with the principles stated in the previous chapter, you have a recipe for success. I am going to give you some examples, but you need to read these passages in your bible for yourself.

Our first example is found in the book of Numbers (Numbers 11:4-6, 31-33). The story begins in the desert where the children of Israel are living on a diet of manna. Manna was clearly God's choice of food for his children. But there was a small group of troublemakers amongst God's people who had a problem with appetite and a lusting for flesh food. These troublemakers stirred up the general populace enough to convince them that what God had given them was not good enough. The New King James Version says: "Who will give us meat to eat" and the New Century Version says: "We want meat". Many people were asking God for something that they knew was against God's better judgment. Never mind the fact that if they had a positive mental attitude and the perseverance that so many self improvement books advocate then they would soon be in the promised land where pomegranate and fig trees grew as far as the eye could see. Never mind the fact that if words of encouragement were given instead of words of discouragement then they would soon be rewarded with clusters of grapes so big that it would take a chainsaw or machete to harvest them! Eating manna was not an unpleasant experience, but it was a temporary fix until something much better in the future was to be experienced. God had big plans for his people, and the time that they were now in was like a test. If they could pass the test then they could reap the reward. The children of Israel instead choose the path of rebellion and complaining, so God answered their prayer in a big way. Quail flew in and landed on the ground all around them and covered the earth for a day's journey in every direction. Not only that, but the quail was three feet deep! We have to be careful; God has a habit of answering our petitions in a big way. If we focus our attention on what what's best for us then we will get it. If on the other hand we focus our attention on what in not good for us then we will get that too. We have to remember that a lot of Israelites died from eating quail. The name of the place where the Israelites died in the Hebrew language is *Qibrôth Hatta'awah* which means "Graves of lust" or "Graves of wanting". We see here that God gave them what they wanted even though it was not what he wanted. This is how generous God is.

Our second example is found in 1 Samuel chapters 8 through 10. The children of Israel came to the prophet Samuel and said "Give us a king so that we can be like all the other nations" this was clearly a request against the wishes of God (1Sam. 12:17, 19). God himself said "They have rejected me from being their king."(NCV) So what did God do? He gave them exactly what they wanted. They wanted tall, dark, and hansom, so God gave them the tallest, darkest, and handsomest man in all the land. Saul was a head taller than everybody else in Israel. Practically overnight Saul went from being an unknown to being the most popular man in Israel. Even though it was God who choose Saul to be king, he relented and said "I am sorry I made Saul king, because he has stopped following me and had not obeyed my commands."NCV (1 Sam 15:11) In the end, the request to have a king turned out to be a tragedy. Saul turned from God, consulted a sorceress, and killed himself. The Philistines cut off

Saul's head and displayed his armor in the pagan temple of a pagan god. It turned out that good looks will only take you so far. From this we can learn that not only do individuals need to be careful what they ask for, nations do too. Even though it caused God great pain, God gave them what they asked for. This is how generous God is.

Our third example is found in Mark 10:2-12. The Pharisees are trying to trick Jesus by bringing up the subject of divorce. In response to their question, Jesus said "what did Moses command you to do?"(NCV) The Pharisees admitted that Moses allowed divorce. Jesus then explained that divorce was not he wanted, but allowed because the Israelites were so stubborn. The Israelites had asked for something that God did not want them to have, and God gave it to them! This is how generous God is.

The forth example of the generous nature of God is found in Luke chapter 8:26-33. This story happened on the shores of the southeast corner of Lake Galilee. Jesus had just gotten out of the boat when he was approached by a man possessed with very many demons. As Jesus was casting out the demons, the demons begged that they be allowed to go into the pigs that were feeding on a nearby hillside. Jesus graciously answered their petition. If god will give demons what they want then how much more will he give us what we want? Demons were never called the children of

God because they were not made in his image. We were made in his image and are called his children (see Eph.1:3-5). For this reason we have more of a reason to expect what we ask for than other beings of the universe, but ironically humans have the most doubt. This doubt is unfounded and without cause. One reason why this book was written was to inspire more faith by giving a logical reason to have more faith. This leads us to the original nature of mankind.

Human Nature

Because I was in the military, I like to give military and intelligence analogies. When an unknown device from a foreign country is found, the military does several things. The first thing is to call experts in from several fields to analyze the device. While the device is being analyzed several question are being asked. One of which is "What was this device designed for?" Was it designed as an offensive weapon, or an intelligence gathering device? It doesn't take a lot of observation to notice that and automobile was designed for transportation. When humans are subjected to this kind of observation the most primary characteristics observed are sensory in nature. Humans have many senses such as taste, touch, sight, hearing, smell, and so on, but all these have one thing in common. The basic design of all sensory organs on humans is for pleasure. God made his offspring to live a life of abundance and pleasure. This is the way it was until mankind sinned. We were not designed primarily to experience depression, sadness, pain, anxiety or fear. I believe that Adam and Eve never experienced a thought that was negative or counterproductive until they had sinned. Likewise we can place ourselves in a very favorable position, similar to Adam and Eve before sin occupied our planet, by simply controlling our thoughts. Think about this: If the law of attraction can get a new house or automobile for me then why can I not leave this planet? Look at what happened to Enoch. If you were just about the only righteous person on a planet full of wicked people, wouldn't you think a lot about leaving the planet? Remember that Jesus said that all things were possible. I propose that Enoch was a man that thought outside of the box. Have you ever noticed that the possibility of Eve having pain during childbirth did not exist in she had sinned. Notice also that after Cain's sin the earth was cursed and man had to work for a living. God s original plan for man was one of leisure and fun. Before sin, Adam and Eve never did anything that they did not want to do. The kind of abundance and carefree living that God had designed for mankind is almost incomprehensible in our present condition. There are too many false beliefs in religious society to allow for that kind of God to exist. Nevertheless God's original design for humans was one of pleasure, abundance, prosperity and advancement beyond anything that we can now comprehend. It is only logical that the restoration process that God has planned for us will bring mankind closer to our original pre-sin state. God's desire for us to enjoy pleasure eternally is so strong that he allows painful events and circumstances to shape our character so that we will be prepared to accept all that he plans to give us.

Chapter Ten

Meditation

Many years ago I studied meditation only to find out that the conservative religious community frowned on the subject. At that time transcendental meditation was being associated with astral projection and Satan worship. I was told to not pursue meditation and to concentrate on important things like paying tithe and getting a proper Christian education. The stern resistance I received from the local religious community prompted me to find out what the Bible really said about meditation. What I found was that the Bible says quite a bit about the subject and in a good way too. The one person in the Bible who speaks most about meditation is David. I can't help but think that all those years he spent as a youth herding sheep must have provided a lot of opportunity to meditate and prepare his mind for a future full of abundance and adventure. David wasn't perfect, but he was on the right side. If he can screw up and come out on top then so can we. We can learn from his mistakes and live a more righteous life than he. David emphasizes meditation. Meditation must have been the vehicle he used to control his thoughts in such a way as to manifest the life he lived. David also mentions the Law, or statutes a lot in connection with meditation. Some theologians debate the Biblical meaning of law, books of the law, and statutes. I too have had to wrestle with this. Generally there are three interpretations of these: the Ten Commandments, the laws of the universe such as the law of attraction, and the Pentateuch (the first five books of the Bible). I have decided that David collectively meant all three because in some verses he contextually points to one interpretation more than the others. But don't take my word for it, read for yourself and decide. Also the context in which the word meditate is used is not always one of a deep trancelike state, but one of contemplative thought. The Bible associates meditation with prosperity and respect for God. The apostle Paul gives us eight criteria or guidelines for us to use when meditating. Let's look at these now.

Philippians 4:8 NKJV

"Finally, brethren, whatever things are true, whatever things are noble, whatever things are just, whatever things are pure, whatever things are lovely, whatever things are of good report, if there is any virtue and if there is anything praiseworthy—**meditate on these things**."

Now let's read the same passage (actually verses eight and nine) in the message Bible and see what additional information can be perceived.

Philippians 4:8-9 MSG

"Summing it all up, friends, I'd say you'll do best by filling your minds and meditating on things true, noble, reputable, authentic, compelling, gracious—the best, not the worst; the beautiful, not the ugly; things to praise, not things to curse. Put into practice what you learned from me, what you heard and saw and realized. Do that, and God, who makes everything work together, will work you into his most excellent harmonies."

There is a lot I could say about this, but I am not going to. There is actually more in this verse than most people see the first few times they read it. Some people don't see it at all. That is the way the Bible is. "The wicked shall do wickedly; and none of the wicked shall understand, but the wise shall **understand**." Daniel 12:9-10. Contrary to what some advocate, there are deep mysteries in scripture that we have not even begin to understand.

Psalm 49:3 NKJV

"My mouth shall speak wisdom, and the **meditation** of my heart shall give **understanding**."

Joshua 1:8 NIV

"Do not let this Book of the Law depart from your mouth; **meditate** on it day and night, so that you may be careful to do everything written in it. Then you will be **prosperous and successful**."

Malachi 3:16 NKJV

"Then those who feared the LORD spoke to one another, And the LORD listened and heard them; So a book of remembrance was written before Him For those who fear the LORD And who **meditate** on His name."

In this verse, the word meditate is synonymous with honor or respect.

Psalm 119:15 NKJV

"I will **meditate** on Your precepts, and contemplate Your ways."

Psalm 119:78, 23 NKJV

"Let the proud be ashamed, for they treated me wrongfully with falsehood; but I will meditate on Your precepts. 23Princes also sit and speak against me, but Your servant **meditates** on Your statutes."

Psalm 1:1-2 NASB

"How blessed is the man who does not walk in the counsel of the wicked, nor stand in the path of sinners, nor sit in the seat of scoffers! 2But his delight is in the law of the LORD, and in His law he **meditates** day and night."

Psalm 119:97, 99 NIV

"Oh, how I love your law! I **meditate** on it all day long. I have more insight than all my teachers, for I **meditate** on your statutes."

Psalm 119:148 NIV

"My eyes stay open through the watches of the night, that I may **meditate** on your promises."

I believe it is good to get out in nature and meditate, and that is what I think about when I read these next two verses.

Psalm 77:12 NCV

"I will **meditate** on all your works and consider all your mighty deeds."

Psalm 145:5 NKJV

"I will **meditate** on the glorious splendor of Your majesty, and on Your wondrous works."

These last few verses are in the context of prayer.

Psalm 5:1 NKJV

"Give ear to my words, O LORD, consider my **meditation**."

Psalm 19:4 NASB

"Let the words of my mouth and the **meditation** of my heart be acceptable in Your sight, O LORD, my rock and my Redeemer."

Psalm 64:1 NKJV

"Hear my voice, O God, in my **meditation**; preserve my life from fear of the enemy."

Psalm 104:34 NIV

"May my **meditation** be pleasing to him, as I rejoice in the LORD."

As we can see the Bible fully supports the practice of meditation, but the word meditation itself can have more than one meaning. Some Christians still stigmatize the art of transcendental meditation because it was derived from the Vedic traditions of India. Still others do the same to the vipassana meditation technique because it was originated by Gotama Buddha, and also because the practice forbids fasting and prayer during the initial training session. Every major religion seems to have its own form of meditation. Despite the differences in theology and philosophy that existed when the Bible was being written, David and many others mentioned in scripture found that going to a place of solitude and practicing the art of sensory deprivation to enhance focus and thought played a key role in their self improvement.

Chapter Eleven

Putting it all together

To summarize all that we have covered so far, and some items we have not covered, let's begin with **asking**. More important, who are we asking. We are asking someone who loves us and is more generous than any human alive, in fact, if you found a person on earth as generous as God, that person would probably be considered a fool. The apostle Paul said "We are fools for Christ's sake," (1Cor.4:10). The closer Paul came to God, the more out of harmony he became to common people. Paul's belief system changed so much, he became a different person, and so can we. After all, who in their right mind would sing praises and give thanks to God after being falsely accused of a crime, beaten many times with a rod, and thrown in prison.(see Acts 16:22-25) Are we so full of gratitude that we would do the same?

We must have faith. We must **believe** that we have what we ask for. We can confidently do this because we know what kind of person God is. As we are asking, we are believing. Also, **as** we are asking **we know God hears** us. Asking and believing are a team. Asking and believing is not so much a single occurrence as they are a lifestyle. Paul says we are to pray without ceasing. As we do this, opportunities will come to us that will enable us to live our life as we desire.

We must **receive** those opportunities and take full advantage of them in order for to manifest what we asked for. For example, I know of a couple who wanted to sell their house. For years they planned, thought, prayed and dressed the yard up nicely until a miracle happened. Out of the blue a man showed up and said "I will give you more money for this house than you can imagine!" What happened next defies logic. The couple ran this man off like a dirty dog, and came to me to complain that they don't get any opportunities in life! This is not the first time this scenario has happened to this couple. The truth is that this couple has had hundreds of similar occurrences and as yet are still living a poverty lifestyle hoping that God will somehow throw a million dollars their way. Despite being blessed with a lot of opportunities, some people still choose to live a life of poverty while still looking for the pot of gold at the end of a rainbow.

They don't see that the pot of gold had been offered to them many times.

Persist in asking, believing, and receiving. Remember that we are to pray without ceasing. The powers of the subconscious are swayed by REPEATED input from the conscious mind. We must tell ourselves repeatedly "I am a child of the king of the universe and no one is more generous than he" We must persist in our contemplation of the fact of our enormous worth and virtually unlimited resources within ourselves for prosperity and goodness toward others. We can bless all we come into contact with, be it man or beast. We must persist in telling ourselves "I believe" and "I know I have a bright future ahead of me" persist in the acknowledgement of the fact that the God of the universe is looking at you right now and will not let anything come into your life except it is for your ultimate prosperity and wellbeing. We must also persist in an attitude of gratitude.

Thankfulness is the proper expression of the soul when we slightly resist the blessings of God. You know that what we resist persist. It is like when someone is trying to pay you money for a job that you intend to do for free, and when you try to turn the money down, they make you take it anyway. Every time the smallest blessing from God or man comes to us we should automatically think that "that's too much". We do this because we are always trying to comprehend the fact that God is in the process of giving us more prosperity than we can imagine, and we expect that at any given moment a large supply (too large in fact) of it is going to be dumped onto us and we will not have the capacity to absorb it. It is almost like having a fear of being blessed too much. I know of a Christian missionary who was being persecuted for his faith in a foreign country and did not complain of his circumstances despite going without food for two weeks. When visiting a friend, the friend offered the missionary a tomato and a cucumber because that is all he had at the time. Upon receiving the food the missionary dropped to his knees and wept out of gratitude. This man was more thankful for a tomato and a cucumber than most others are when they buy a new car. Let us not forget what the Bible says about this. "in everything give thanks; for this is God's will for you in Christ Jesus." (14)

Let us not forget **the extreme generosity of God**. There is a parable in the Bible (Matt. 25:14-30) of three servants who were given money (wealth, blessing) by their master. One was given five talents, one two talents, and the last servant was given one talent. The first two put their money in circulation where it could do others some good. The last servant hid his one talent out of **fear**. When the traveling master returned from a journey he asked the servant that had one talent what had become of the money and why. The answer given was "I know that you are this type of person". The servant then goes on to give a description of our father number one and accuse the master of being that type of person. The answer given by the master is interesting. It is like God telling us that he will be any kind of God that we want him to be, but falsely accusing God of being a person that he really is not will make him angry. Notice that the servant that had a false view of the character and generosity of his master ended up being cast into outer darkness. Let us not act out of fear, but be confidently thankful for the tremendous blessings that God is about to bestow upon us.

Just imagine that we are all fish swimming in an ocean of **wealth and prosperity**. In reality, that is the way it is. After the flood, Noah looked out to see that the lush exotic world which he had known all of his life had been replaced with mud and rotting corpuses of billions of people, dinosaurs, and animals. If there was any sight that would drive a man to drinking, this was it. Without any effort from any human the earth has recovered from this catastrophe. This is because God has designed the universe to constantly prosper and rebuild itself. Think about this: unless mankind interferes with the natural order of things on earth or elsewhere, there is always a natural progression toward prosperity. To word it more plainly; things are always changing for the better. We just have to learn to live our lives in harmony with God and nature to prosper as God intended us to. The law of attraction is just part of this. God never meant for humans to be negative and pessimistic. At this point in time God will not force wealth on us; we can choose not to be wealthy if we so desire. There is a story in the Bible about a man named Agur. (Proverbs 30) Agur asked God to not make him rich or poor. Agur did not want to be poor because he would be tempted to steal and therefore would displease God. He also did not want to be rich because this (he feared) would cause him to forget God much the same way Saul forgot God. I believe Agur was a righteous; God fearing man, but he also had too little faith in his relationship with God. If someone was so weak as to let wealth come in-between them and God; did they have a close relationship with God to begin with? The Bible is very clear that a relationship with God take precedence over any amount of material wealth.

Proverbs 28:6 NCV

"It is better to be poor and innocent than to be rich and wicked."

Obviously not every rich person is wicked, nor is every poor person innocent. If you take a wicked person that has never known God, and has no desire to live according to the laws of God, and give them an enormous amount of wealth; that wealth will keep that person from **seeing their need** to walk with God. The truth is that monetary wealth can be a blessing or a curse. I hope in your case it will be a blessing.

There is a story in the book of Second Chronicles chapter twenty that we need to be familiar with. It's a story of a serious threat and the end result of what happens when a group of people follows the principles you have just read about. You can read the story in your Bible; I will be quoting from the New Century version. The story starts out with three nations banding together to annihilate the kingdom of Judah which included the city of Jerusalem. Messengers had been dispatched to inform King Jehoshaphat that the Moabites, Ammonites, and Edomites (Meunites) had combined forces and was heading in his direction. King Jehoshaphat was very afraid because he knew he did not stand a chance against so large an army. The king, feeling that there was only one option; decided to "**ask** the Lord what to do" He then decided to proclaim a nationwide "**fast** during this special time of **prayer** to God." Then the whole kingdom "came together to **ask** the Lord for help" Nothing gets people in the spirit of asking like a crisis. Have you considered that if people were always in a spirit of prayer to begin with, then God may not have allowed the crisis to come at all? Jehoshaphat and the kingdom of Judah were desperate; they searched the archives for a promise from God they could use to save them in their hour of need. They didn't even have a prayer to pray, they had to go find one! What they found was the prayer Solomon prayed at the dedication of the temple. The prayer (1Kings 8:30-40) was a request that anyone in distress could go to the temple, or face the temple, confess God's name, turn from their sins, and God would save them. Jehoshaphat and all Judah prayed this prayer as a promise, the fact that this request became a promise is mentioned in Glenn Coons book "The A, B, Cs of Bible Prayer" (page 95). The sin that Judah had to atone for was one that took place some six hundred years before. God gave a strict warning not to let any of the inhabitants of Cana live when conquering the land. (Num.33:52, 55; Deut.7:2) Because the Ammonites. Moabites, and Edomites were not destroyed over half a century before, Judah was now reaping the harvest of disobedience. When Judah prayed they said "We will cry out to you when we are in trouble. Then **you will hear and save us**." The people believed that God was going to hear their prayer and was going to save them. Then the Spirit of God entered a man named Jahaziel and caused him to say something positive and encouraging. He said "**Don't be afraid** or discouraged because of this large army. The battle is not your battle, it is God's.... Just stand strong in your places, and you will see the lord save you. Judah and Jerusalem don't be afraid or discouraged, because the lord is with you." Upon hearing this Jehoshaphat bowed his face to the ground in **gratitude**. Upon seeing Jehoshaphat bow, all of Judah bowed face down to the ground in gratitude. Then the Levites stood up and "**praised the Lord**, the god of Israel, with very loud voices." If your enemy was fixing to slaughter you, would you feel like singing praises? The next morning Jehoshaphat stood up and said "**Have faith** in the Lord your God, and you will stand strong. Have faith in his prophets, and **you will succeed**." He then chooses certain men to be singers to sing the victory song. In ancient times after a battle, the winner would sing a victory song as they headed back home. Jehoshaphat gave the command for the victory song to be sung in anticipation of the **expected victory that was theirs through faith**. They sang "Thank the Lord, because his love continues forever" Here they are thanking the lord for the victory before the battle has even begun! The story goes on to say that "**As** they begin to sing and praise God", God caused the Ammonites and Moabites to attack and kill the Edomites. The Ammonites and Moabites then attacked each other until no one was left alive. Think about this: if it came down to two people, one Ammonite, and one Moabite; they would have to simultaneously inflict a fatal wound on each other for this to happen the way the Bible says it did. Judah, led by King Jehoshaphat, marched through a ravine into the Desert of Jeruel ready for battle only to find dead bodies as far as the eye could see. God not only gave them victory, but also gave them prosperity too. There were so many valuables in the camp of the enemy; it took three days to gather up all the loot. On the forth day Jehoshaphat and his army met in a valley and praised the Lord. That is why the valley today is called the Valley of Beracah which means "valley of praise" or "valley of blessing". This story stands out as one of the very few in which people used the principles of success found in scripture and in so many self help books. I think the result speaks for itself.

Is it possible that everyday is actually a great day with unlimited possibilities for adventure and everything else is an illusion? Is it possible that people suffering from depression and anxiety are actually living in paradise and they don't even know it? Every time the apostle Paul suffered privation and persecution he rejoiced and gave thanks. What did he know that most people don't? Circumstances should never affect our happiness for the worse, but for the better. Optimists have only a forward gear and two speeds: fast and faster. Because of Romans 8: 28, Christians have a reason (and obligation) to rejoice when circumstances take a turn for the worse. Let's stop right now and read Romans 8:28 and some other verses that you have just read and let them sink in.

And we know that all things work together for good to those who love God, to those who are the called according to His purpose. NKJV

We live by what we believe, not by what we can see. NCV

And whatsoever things you ask in prayer, believing, you will receive. NKJV

I tell you to believe that you have received the things you ask for in prayer, and God will give them to you. NCV

All things are possible for the one who believes. NCV

If you ask me for anything in my name, I will do it. NCV

We do not look at the things which are seen, but at the things which are not seen. NKJV

Psalm 23 has never been one of my favorite verses of scripture, but in closing I want you to read it slowly in the Message Bible. While you are reading it, imagine sheep sitting around a table having a meal while wolves watch close by. The sheep don't care. The Shepherd is close by with his trusty Shepherd's rod. The wolves being a threat are just an illusion.

1-3 God, my shepherd! I don't need a thing.

You have bedded me down in lush meadows,
you find me quiet pools to drink from.

True to your word,

you let me catch my breath

and send me in the right direction.

⁴ Even when the way goes through

Death Valley,

I'm not afraid

when you walk at my side.

Your trusty shepherd's crook

makes me feel secure.

⁵ You serve me a six-course dinner

right in front of my enemies.

You revive my drooping head;

my cup brims with blessing.

⁶ Your beauty and love chase after me

every day of my life.

I'm back home in the house of GOD

for the rest of my life.

Recommended Reading

The Bible

A Happy Pocket Full of Money, by David Cameron Gikandi

How to Win Friends & Influence People, by Dale Carnegie

It's Not About The Money, by Bob Proctor

See You At The Top, by Zig Ziglar

The Power of Positive Thinking, by Norman Vincent Peale

Your Best Life Now, by Joel Osteen

How to Develop Self-Confidence & Influence People by Public Speaking, by Dale Carnegie

The Quick & Easy Way to Effective Speaking, by Dale Carnegie

Thought Vibrations, by William Atkinson

The Key: The Missing Secret For Attracting Anything You Want, by Joe Vitale

Acres of Diamonds, by Russell Conwell

Wealth Beyond Reason, by Bob Doyle

How to Stop Worrying and Start Living, by Dale Carnegie

You Were Born Rich, by Bob Proctor

Think and Grow Rich, by Napoleon Hill

Excuses Begone!, by Dr. Wayne Dyer

Change your thoughts; Change your life, by Dr. Wayne Dyer

Happy for No Reason, by Marci Shimoff

Success Through a Positive Mental, Attitude By Napoleon Hill and W. Clement Stone

The magic of Believing, by Claude Bristol

Be Rich!, by Robert Collier

Secret of the Ages, by Robert Collier

The Amazing Secrets of the Far East, by Robert Collier

The Secret of Power, by Robert Collier

Prayer Works! By Robert Collier

The Power of Your Subconscious Mind, by Joseph Murphy

The Law of the Higher Potential, by Robert Collier

The Magic Word, by Robert Collier

The God in You, by Robert Collier

The Master Key System, by Charles Haanel

The Amazing secrets of the Yogi, by Charles Haanel

The Hidden Power, by Thomas Troward

Affirmations: things to write and say

The power of choice

I choose to be abundant

I choose to be kind

I choose to be serene

I choose to be generous

I choose to be gratefulc

I choose to be supportive

I choose to be happy

I choose to be joyful

I choose to prosper

I choose to be pure and righteous

I choose to be positive and encouraging

I choose to believe

I choose to enjoy all things

I choose to be secure

The power of being

I am abundant and prosperous

I am kind and gracious

I am grateful

I am happy

I am joyful

I am pure and righteous

I am positive

I am wealth

I am joy

I am serene

I am tranquil

I am peaceful

I am benevolent

I am love

I am thankful

The power of life

I live in an ocean of love

I live in an ocean of peace

I live in an ocean of abundance

I live in an ocean of serenity

I live in an ocean of calm

I live in an ocean of plenty

I live in an ocean of happiness

I live in an ocean of security

I live in an ocean of wealth

I live in an ocean of joy

I live in an ocean of unlimited opportunities

I live in an ocean of boundless adventure

Endnotes

1. The Power of Positive Thinking, Page 172
2. Think and Grow Rich, Pages 50
3. ibid, Page 46
4. Hebrews 11:6, New International Version
5. Think and Grow Rich, Page 212
6. ibid, Page 52
7. ibid, Page 53
8. ibid, Page 72
9. Proverbs 4:23, New Century Version
10. Think and Grow Rich, Page 49
11. ibid, page 57
12. ibid, page 93-94
13. ibid, page 27
14. 1 Thessalonians 5:18, New American Standard Version

Self-Help and the Bible
Volume 2

Contents

Preface

The brevity of volume one of this series has raised more questions than it has answered. Trying to reconcile humanistic views of the law of attraction with the Bible has put me in an awkward position. In volume one I showed the similarities between the Bible and the material on the popular book and DVD titled "The Secret". I however do not agree with the all the views others have on the law of attraction, and for this reason I have written this book. There are so many important self-help topics not covered in volume one that I feel compelled to bring them to your attention in this volume. I believe that any self-help topic emphasized in scripture warrants our attention. There are still some self-help related topics that I will not put in writing, but will only discuss them orally. Such topics such as the ancient techniques used to amplify brain wave signals for the purposes of manifestation or levitation will not be in my books because it is easier to talk about such subjects than it is write about them. As with all of my books, a variety of scripture will be quoted and a large font point will be used. I have also taken the liberty to bold key words and phrases to emphasize a point dealing with the subject. Keep in mind that this book was not written to answer all your questions, but to inspire thought. You may have even more questions after reading this. In our quest to find the truth we may have to consider many arguments and hear many points of view. The subjects presented in this volume are not new to the self-improvement industry; I just give scripture to support or refute the premise. I also must express deep gratitude and acknowledgement to the book titled "Charles F. Kettering A Biography" by Thomas Alvin Boyd. This book was inspirational and a very helpful for material in the second chapter. I recommend this book for those seeking more detail than what I give in this volume. The last chapter of this book has nothing to do with the subject, so just disregard it. It was written for the few chosen to read it, and they know who they are.

Chapter One

The Law of Attraction

Ecclesiastes 6:10 NCV

"**Whatever happens was planned long ago**. Everyone knows what people are like. No one can argue with God, who is stronger than anyone."

I don't feel comfortable writing about this subject. I believe there is a lot about this that is not being discussed. I do not agree with some views on the law of attraction because they describe God as impersonal, or they describe the law of attraction as the art of manipulating God to give you what you want. When I wrote about this before, I used the story of Job as an example of the law of attraction. The truth is that what happened to Job was so extreme that the law of attraction as expounded by many self-help gurus

1

could not have accounted for all that had happened to Job. The first chapter of Job makes it clear that supernatural forces outside our realm were responsible for Job's misfortune regardless of what Job was thinking. In fact, the Bible says there was no cause for the misfortune of Job.

Job 2:3 AMP

"And the Lord said to Satan, Have you considered My servant Job, that there is none like him on the earth, a blameless and upright man, one who [reverently] fears God and abstains from and shuns all evil [because it is wrong]? And still he holds fast his integrity, although you moved Me against him to destroy him **without cause**."

The question to ask may be "Am I to control my circumstances, or my reaction to my circumstances?" Do we dare claim victory over our circumstances and take credit for them after knowing that king Nebuchadnezzar was punished for doing the same?(Daniel 4:30-33) Nebuchadnezzar learned the hard way that God gets the credit for our prosperity and not man. Self-help tells us that the strength we need and the answers we seek are within. We are told to focus within ourselves. Jesus always taught that our focus is to be on God, the source of all strength and answers. These two views may be harmonized by accepting the fact that God lives in us if we let Him. God and Satan both work through human agencies. What do we say to the Jews that perished during world war two? Do we say "It's your fault for using the law of attraction to bring this upon yourselves!" These are the issues that we have to deal with when we consider the law of attraction. Mel Gibson made Christianity more real when he made the movie "The Passion of the Christ" The movie depicted realistically what it was like to get thirty nine lashes with a whip. I keep this in mind when I ponder the life of Paul. Paul's life changed dramatically after his conversion. Before his conversion Paul's life was considered prosperous, normal, and successful from a worldly point of view. After his conversion Paul was persecuted in every way possible (2 Corinthians 11:24-27). Paul suffered from hunger, thirst, sleeplessness, was stoned and left for dead, was beaten with rods three times, was shipwrecked three times, and five times received the thirty-nine lashes depicted in Mel Gibson's movie. Here is the question. Did Paul use the law of attraction to bring all of this persecution upon himself or were there supernatural forces outside his control directing his circumstances? If our thoughts determine our circumstances, what thoughts did Paul have to have to bring such bad luck upon himself? Or are our circumstances totally overseen by Gods permissive will? If we ponder this thoroughly we may see that God is a little bit bigger than we previously thought. Here is another question.

How do we reconcile the law of attraction with 2 Timothy 3:12? In the New King James version it simply states that " all who desire to live godly in Christ Jesus will suffer persecution". Just what are all these Godly people doing to bring persecution upon themselves? Are Gods people unable to think happy thoughts to attract happy circumstances to themselves? Just incase there is a misunderstanding, let's read 2 Timothy 3:12 in some other versions.

NCV

"Everyone who wants to live as God desires, in Christ Jesus, will be persecuted."

CEV

"Anyone who belongs to Christ Jesus and wants to live right will have trouble from others."

AMP

"Indeed all who delight in piety and are determined to live a devoted and godly life in Christ Jesus will meet with persecution [will be made to suffer because of their religious stand]."

GW

"Those who try to live a godly life because they believe in Christ Jesus will be persecuted."

You also might try reading this in the Message Bible. The Bible doesn't say that the persecuted are guilty of bringing persecution upon themselves because they used the law of attraction to attract hostile circumstances. The Bible seems to imply that no matter what we think and do, if we think and do as God wants us to, we will be persecuted. While it seems very appealing to think that we are in total control of our circumstances; scripture seems to indicate that the supernatural forces of good and evil take precedent over what we think and do. Daniel's three friends referred to commonly by their Babylonian names as Shadrach, Meshach, and Abed-Nego experienced a stressful situation due to a choice they had made. Do we say that they used the law of attraction to attract being thrown into a fiery furnace? Do we say that Daniel used the law of attraction to attract being thrown into a den of hungry lions? Or did Daniel do and think as God would have him to, and as a result was persecuted?

Let's consider the circumstances Jonah encountered. God created a big fish to swallow Jonah for the purposes of preserving his life and transporting him 560 + miles to Nineveh (Jonah 1:17). Did Jonah attract being swallowed by a big fish or not. If he did then we can too right? It's just a matter of thought. Many self-help advocates say we can control our circumstances while the Bible says that God controls our circumstances. Can both views be correct at the same time? Some self-help people say that we control what God does by our thoughts, and that this is the law of attraction. Somehow the thought of humans controlling God doesn't seem right. The major theme of scripture is that God is in control. We always have the power of choice, but God controls the universe.

Proverbs 16:1 NCV

"People may make plans in their minds, but only the Lord can make them come true."

Let's look at the law of attraction through First Kings chapter seventeen. In chapter three we will discuss the first half of the chapter, but for this subject we need only to examine the last half. You may want to read the whole chapter for context. Elijah is staying at a woman's house; and she has a son that gets sick and dies. This is verses nineteen and twenty in the New Century Version.

"Elijah said to her, "Give me your son." Elijah took the boy from her, carried him upstairs, and laid him on the bed in the room where he was staying.20 Then he prayed to the Lord: "Lord my God, this widow is letting me stay in her house. **Why have you done this terrible thing to her and caused her son to die**?"

God is clearly being blamed for the painful circumstance that is affecting Elijah and the family he is staying with. The ancient Greeks have always depicted gods or supernatural forces as manipulators of the circumstances of mankind. This brings us to **choice and chance**. We always have a choice, and our choices do affect our destiny. Despite our power of choice, it is God that initiates the action that propels us to our destiny.

Romans 9:14-18 MSG

"Is that grounds for complaining that God is unfair? Not so fast, please. God told Moses, "I'm in charge of mercy. I'm in charge of compassion." Compassion doesn't originate in our bleeding hearts or moral sweat, but in God's mercy. The same point was made when God said to Pharaoh, "I picked you as a bit player in this drama of my salvation power." All we're saying is that **God has the first word, initiating the action in which we play our part for good or ill**."

Let us read verse 16 in the Amplified Version to get a clearer understanding of what is being said.

"So then [God's gift] is not a question of human will and human effort, but of God's mercy. [It depends not on one's own willingness nor on his strenuous exertion as in running a race, but on God's having mercy on him.]"

So much for human will and human effort, the Bible repeatedly points to the will of God as governing our circumstances and not the will of man. What would happen if the will of man worked in harmony with the will of God?

1 Samuel 16:8 MSG

"Jesse then called up Abinadab and presented him to Samuel. Samuel said, "This man isn't **God's choice** either."

Regardless of the thoughts of Abinadab or David, it was God's choice was that David was to be king and not Abinadab. What does the Bible say about chance playing a part in our future circumstances?

2 Kings 24:2 MSG

"**God dispatched** a succession of raiding bands against him: Babylonian, Aramean, Moabite, and Ammonite. The strategy was to destroy Judah. Through the preaching of his servants and prophets, God had said he would do this, and now he was doing it. **None of this was by chance—it was God's judgment** as he turned his back on Judah because of the enormity of the sins of Manasseh—Manasseh, the killer-king, who made the Jerusalem streets flow with the innocent blood of his victims. God wasn't about to overlook such crimes."

Even the pagan and secular powers of this world were controlled by God and they never knew it. Countless nations in history who never knew God had no idea that they were mere puppets to be used as God wills. Pagans as well as Jews and Christians have always wondered how much of life was a result of chance and how much was divine providence. We see this in a story told in First Samuel chapters four through six about the Ark of the Covenant as it was captured by the Philistines. The Philistines suffered terribly from what most Bible scalars interpret as something like hemorrhoids or tumors. The decision was made that God had sent the painful plague, and to return the ark to Israel with a penalty offering. The ark was loaded into a new cart drawn by two oxen and set loose toward the Israelite city of Beth Shemesh. Let's see what First Samuel chapter six verse nine has to say in the New Century Version.

"Watch the cart. If it goes toward Beth Shemesh in Israel's own land, the Lord has given us this great sickness. But if it doesn't, we will know that Israel's God has not punished us. Our sickness **just happened by chance**."

The oxen took the cart to Beth Shemesh as a sign that their circumstances were of divine origin and not by chance. Now let us look at what Solomon had to say about chance and God controlling the fate of his people.

Ecclesiastes 9:1-2, 11 NCV

"I thought about all this and tried to understand it. I saw that **God controls good people and wise people and what they do**, but no one knows if they will experience love or hate.2 Good and bad people end up the same— those who are right and those who are wrong, those who are good and those who are evil, those who are clean and those who are unclean, those who sacrifice and those who do not. The same things happen to a good person as happen to a sinner, to a person who makes promises to God and to one who does not."

"11 I also saw something else here on earth: The fastest runner does not always win the race, the strongest soldier does not always win the battle, the wisest does not always have food, the smartest does not always become wealthy, and the talented one does not always receive praise. **Time and chance happen to everyone.**"

Verse one is topically related to Romans 8:28 and is so important to this subject that I devoted chapter four entirely to Romans 8:28.

Now we need to look at the prosperity enjoyed by Hezekiah King of Judah. The Bible says in the last sentence of verse thirty of Second Chronicles chapter thirty two that "…Hezekiah prospered in all that he did." (NASB). What did Hezekiah do to attract so much wealth? Did he think thoughts of prosperity and abundance?

2 Chronicles 32:26-29 NASB

"However, **Hezekiah humbled the pride of his heart**, both he and the inhabitants of Jerusalem, so that the wrath of the LORD did not come on them in the days of Hezekiah. [27]Now Hezekiah had immense riches and honor; and he made for himself treasuries for silver, gold, precious stones, spices, shields and all kinds of valuable articles, [28]storehouses also for the produce of grain, wine and oil, pens for all kinds of cattle and sheepfolds for the flocks. [29]He made cities for himself and acquired flocks and herds in abundance, **for God had given him very great wealth**."

In scripture prosperity always follows after humility and disaster after pride and self sufficiency. Since God is the source of all prosperity the correct attitude would naturally be one of acknowledging our dependence on God for everything we have, or ever will have. This includes military victories and personal accomplishments. There are more examples of humility and arrogance in the life story of Hezekiah. Listen to what Sennacherib king of Assyria had to say about God just before he attacked Jerusalem.

2 Kings 18:32-37 NCV

"…Don't listen to Hezekiah. He is fooling you when he says, 'The Lord will save us.' 33 **Has a god of any other nation saved his people from the power of the king of Assyria**? 34 Where are the gods of Hamath and Arpad? Where are the gods of Sepharvaim, Hena, and Ivvah? They did not save Samaria from my power.35Not one of all the gods of these countries has saved his people from me. **Neither can the LORD save Jerusalem from my power.**"

Hezekiah's fear is understood in the face of being annihilated by what was then the most powerful nation on earth. Notice Hezekiah's response.

2 Kings 19:14-15 CEV

"After Hezekiah had read the note from the king of Assyria, he took it to the temple and spread it out for the LORD to see. ¹⁵He prayed: LORD God of Israel, your throne is above the winged creatures. **You**

created the heavens and the earth, and you alone rule the kingdoms of this world."

Jerusalem was besieged by the armies of Assyria and death seemed imminent. The King of Assyria has bragged about his past accomplishments and his will to destroy the Jews. Now God steps into the story and gives an encouraging message to Hezekiah through the prophet Isaiah, the son of Amoz

2 Kings 19:20-21, 23-25, 28 NCV

"…I have heard your prayer to me about Sennacherib king of Assyria.21 This is what the Lord has said against Sennacherib:.."

"22 You have insulted me and spoken against me; you have raised your voice against me. You have a proud look on your face, which is against me, the Holy One of Israel.23 You have sent your messengers to insult the Lord. You have said, "With my many chariots I have gone to the tops of the mountains, to the highest mountains of Lebanon. I have cut down its tallest cedars and its best pine trees. I have gone to its farthest places and to its best forests.24 I have dug wells in foreign countries and drunk water there. By the soles of my feet, I have dried up all the rivers of Egypt." 25 "'King of Assyria, surely you have heard. **Long ago I, the Lord, planned these things. Long ago I designed them, and now I have made them**

happen. I allowed you to turn those strong, walled cities into piles of rocks."

"28 Because you rage against me, and because I have heard your proud words, **I will put my hook in your nose and my bit in your mouth**. Then **I will force you to leave my country** the same way you came.'"

God just listed the accomplishments of a wicked worldly king and said "long ago I planned, I designed, and I made them happen". How does the law of attraction fit into God's plans? God's permissive will is found in the last sentence of verse twenty five in the term 'I allow'. I may be proud of some certain accomplishment in my life, but the truth is that I could not have done it without God's help or permission. That is why I cannot be proud of anything I do or accomplish. I am humbly thankful that God allows me to do anything at all. God took care of the Assyrian threat. That night God sent a destroying angel into the Assyrian camp, and the angel slew 185,000 soldiers. The timing of this event cannot be overlooked. 701B.C. was a Jubilee year on the Hebrew calendar, and that night was coincidentally Passover evening. That night the planet Mars passed over the earth thereby changing the orbit of the earth and the time it took the earth to orbit the sun. Before 701 B.C. all calendars reflected the 360 days it took the earth to orbit the sun. This is why there are 360 degrees in a circle: for most of Earth's history we had a 360 day year. Before 701 B.C. Mars had an orbit of 720 days or twice 360, after 701 B.C. the orbit of Mars became 687 days. Since many end time Bible prophecies are set in a 360 day calendar year, something will have to happen to reset our orbit to pre 701 B.C. status.

Most self-help books say that prosperity and poverty alike are the result of thought. The Bible says that for God's people, it is the result of obedience or disobedience to the will and laws of God. The prophet Jeremiah makes this point clear when describing the destruction of Jerusalem by King Nebuchadnezzar of Babylon.

Jeremiah 40:3, 44:2-3 TNIV

"And now the LORD has brought it about; he has done just as he said he would. **All this happened because you people sinned against the LORD and did not obey him**."

"This is what the LORD Almighty, the God of Israel, says: You saw the great disaster I brought on Jerusalem and on all the towns of Judah. **Today they lie deserted and in ruins** [3] **because of the evil they have done**. They aroused my anger by burning incense to and worshiping other gods that neither they nor you nor your ancestors ever knew."

Lamentations 4:13 NCV

"Jerusalem was punished because her prophets and her priests had **sinned** and caused the death of innocent victims."

Disobedience to God can bring sudden calamity. God uses all nations, all religions, and all races to accomplish his purposes. The supernatural forces of the universe ultimately decide who leads the nations of men (see Daniel 2:21, 4:35; Job 12:23-24) Despite all of our war technology, spying, and massive financial resources, it is God who decides what nations have the most influence and rank in the world.

Jeremiah 44:30 TNIV

"This is what the LORD says: '**I am going to deliver Pharaoh Hophra king of Egypt** into the hands of his enemies who seek his life, just as **I gave Zedekiah king of Judah** into the hands of Nebuchadnezzar king of Babylon, the enemy who was seeking his life.' "

Chapters twenty seven and twenty eight of Deuteronomy are noted for explaining the details of the relationship between obedience and prosperity. God rewards disobedience by allowing the harshest environment to envelope society. You can read it for yourself to get all the facts; I will quote a few verses here to show their relevance.

Deuteronomy 28:1-2, 12, 15, 43-44, 47, 54-61 CEV

"1-2Today I am giving you the laws and teachings of the LORD your God. **Always obey them, and the LORD** will make Israel the most famous and important nation on earth, and **he will bless you in many ways**."

"12The LORD will open the storehouses of the skies where he keeps the rain, and he will send rain on your land at just the right times. **He will make you successful in everything you do. You will have plenty of money** to lend to other nations, but you won't need to borrow any yourself."

"15Israel, today I am giving you the laws and teachings of the LORD your God. And **if you don't obey them all**, he will put many curses on you."

"43Foreigners in your towns will become wealthy and powerful, **while you become poor and powerless. 44You will be so short of money that you will have to borrow from those foreigners**. They will be the leaders in the community, and you will be the followers."

"⁴⁷**If the LORD makes you wealthy**, but you don't joyfully worship and honor him, 48he will send enemies to attack you and make you their slaves. Then you will live in poverty with nothing to eat, drink, or wear, and your owners will work you to death."

"54-55Because of hunger, a man who had been gentle and kind will eat his own children and refuse to share the meal with his brother or wife or with his other children. 56-57A woman may have grown up in such luxury that she never had to put a foot on the ground. But times will be so bad that she will secretly eat both her newborn baby and the afterbirth, without sharing any with her husband or her other children. 58You must obey everything in The Book of God's Law. Because if you don't respect the LORD, 59he will punish you and your descendants with incurable diseases, 60like those you were so afraid of in Egypt. 61Remember! **If the LORD decides to destroy your nation**, he can use any disease or disaster, not just the ones written in The Book of God's Law."

How does the book of Deuteronomy influence our views on the Law of Attraction? It seems from what we have read so far that wealth and poverty for God's people is a matter of obedience, or disobedience to his laws (including laws involving choice and thought). Some people though are incredibly evil and wealthy. Does not God let it rain on the just and the unjust? In order for God to be fair, he has to be fair to the just and the unjust. Needless to say, the lifestyle of a nation can go downhill quickly when worldliness replaces godliness. I believe there are many times the supernatural forces of good and evil use prosperity or poverty to test us regardless of what we think or do. On the chessboard of the universe, humans are the pawns. We are rats in a transparent maze that are constantly being tested in every way. Mankind have long sought the secret formula of the correct thoughts to think, or the actions to do to cause the supernatural forces of the universe (good or evil) to grant us the prosperity we so desperately want. The Bible clearly tells us to simply ask. There are no hoops to jump through, and no secret societies to join. Simply follow the steps listed in volume one of this series is all that God asks. There are deep secrets in scripture that no one cares to look at. In light of the law of attraction it would do us well to consider many of our circumstances as tests from above. Here are some reference texts to clarify the biblical position on the subject. Do we control our circumstances through our thoughts, or does God control our circumstances to test our thoughts, or are both true to some extent?

Proverbs 17:3 NASB

"The refining pot is for silver and the furnace for gold, But **the LORD tests hearts**."

Exodus 16:4 TNIV

"Then the LORD said to Moses, "I will rain down bread from heaven for you. The people are to go out each day and gather enough for that day. **In this way I will test them** and see whether they will follow my instructions.""

Exodus 20:18-20 TNIV

"When the people saw the thunder and lightning and heard the trumpet and saw the mountain in smoke, they trembled with fear. They stayed at a distance [19] and said to Moses, "Speak to us yourself and we will listen. But do not have God speak to us or we will die." [20] Moses said to the people, "Do not be afraid. **God has come to test you, so that the fear of God will be with you to keep you from sinning.**""

Deuteronomy 8:2 TNIV

"Remember how the LORD your God led you all the way in the wilderness these forty years, **to humble and test you in order to know what was in your heart**, whether or not you would keep his commands."

Judges 2:20-23 TNIV

"Therefore the LORD was very angry with Israel and said, "Because this nation has violated the covenant I ordained for their ancestors and has not listened to me, 21 I will no longer drive out before them any of the nations Joshua left when he died. 22 **I will use them to test Israel and see whether they will keep the way of the LORD** and walk in it as their ancestors did." 23 The LORD had allowed those nations to remain; he did not drive them out at once by giving them into the hands of Joshua."

1 Chronicles 29:17 TNIV

"I know, my God, **that you test the heart** and are pleased with integrity. All these things have I given willingly and with honest intent. And now I have seen with joy how willingly your people who are here have given to you."

2 Chronicles 32:31 TNIV

"It was Hezekiah who blocked the upper outlet of the Gihon spring and channeled the water down to the west side of the City of David. He succeeded in everything he undertook. 31But when envoys were sent by the rulers of Babylon to ask him about the miraculous sign that had occurred in the land, **God**

left him to test him and to know everything that was in his heart."

Job 7:7, 16-19 NIRV

"7 God, remember that my life is only a breath. I'll never be happy again."

"16 I hate my life. I don't want to live forever. Leave me alone. My days don't mean anything to me. 17 "What are human beings that you think so much of them? What are they that you pay so much attention to them? 18 **You check up on them every morning. You put them to the test every moment**. 19 Won't you ever look away from me? Won't you leave me alone even for one second?"

Jeremiah 20:12 NIRV

"Lord, you rule over all. **You test those who do what is right. You see what is in people's hearts and minds.** So pay them back for what they've done. I've committed my cause to you."

Instead of applying enormous amounts of effort striving to attract wealth, should not God's people focus their attention on a closer relationship with God and accomplishing the purpose they were put on this earth for? What we focus our thoughts on is important. The selfless example of Jesus Christ is not congruent with the materialistic gospel expounded by some Christian ministers. There is just too much scripture emphasizing the powerlessness of mankind, and the necessity of our total dependence upon God for wisdom and strength. I personally believe that the theories that many self-help books advocate border on divination and leave the door open for satanic deception. Haven't Christians learned that it is not our power that we wield, but He who lives in us?

2 Corinthians 12:10 AMP

"So for the sake of Christ, I am well pleased and take pleasure in infirmities, insults, hardships, persecutions, perplexities and distresses; **for when I am weak** [in human strength], **then am I [truly] strong** (able, powerful in divine strength)."

Last thoughts

Now that I have trashed some arguments on the law of attraction and stirred up a hornets nest on the issue, let me state that there are some misunderstandings on this subject. We are not just discussing a secular philosophy on life, but a Christian and possibly universal philosophy as well. So how do we harmonize scripture with the philosophy of the law of attraction? We first must understand that the various aspects of philosophy, theology, and even the environment we live in will seem to disagree with each other because of the way we view them. Many false paradigms work not by giving false information, but by causing incorrect assumptions to be made from facts. One theory that seems to harmonize scripture with the law of attraction is the circles of influence theory. This theory is like describing a wheel within a wheel within a wheel and so on. The theory states that the innermost circle of influence is the realm affected by what we term the law of attraction. This circle is controlled by our thoughts and choices. The outer circles of influence are controlled by supernatural forces. The combination of all circles of influence gives us the circumstances we see in real time. This is an interesting theory and is something to contemplate. It doesn't answer the question of why is the Bible is strangely silent on the sphere of the inner circle of influence. Perhaps to the more enlightened minds of the ancients the subject of what to do with our thoughts and choices seemed too basic to mention. Or perhaps by divine agreement this information was kept hidden from the masses for a specific purpose. When the proper viewpoint is achieved with the facts that we do have then the scriptures presented in this chapter will blend in perfectly with all correct views of philosophy. This is a serious matter. I don't like the term "Law of Attraction" as it seems too much like getting than giving. I prefer to call it something like "The way of Life". I believe most students of the subject may be discussing the same thing, but the differences in terminology confuses the subject, and when religion is involved, that is all it takes to bring accusations of heresy to the table. I will now give you my version of the application of this philosophy.

1. Be totally honest with yourself.

2. Be willing to let go of everything that doesn't support your goal of who God wants you to be. Let go of doubt, fear, worry, depression, and self limitation. Give them all to God. Let go of any inclination to control people or circumstances.

3. Remember that God is in the drivers seat (Matthew 16:24 MSG) and that he is in charge of our circumstances.

4. Have faith and gratitude by accepting the fact that God has a definite purpose for your existence.

5. Spend time every day in prayer/meditation, and reading self-help books, and scripture.

6. Focus your thoughts on your desires and goals not on fears and negative circumstances. We have to focus on "the best, not the worst; the beautiful, not the ugly; things to praise, not things to curse." (see Philippians 4:8-9 MSG)

7. Live a life of expectancy. (Luke 2:25-32; John 3:13-15 MSG) Expect God to guide your steps down the path he has laid out for you. Expect only positive and optimistic outcomes. If you have a problem with this, Joel Osteen has some excellent video material on this at his website.

8. Change your hardwired belief systems through affirmations. Repetitious affirmations when used with persistence will affect the subconscious mind. You can use this method to increase your faith. Use the healing code to heal the spirit thereby making affirmations more effective. (The first two affirmations I started using years ago are found on pages 98 and 99 in Norman Vincent Peal's "The Power of Positive Thinking")

9. Be an extreme optimist. Realize the glass is nether half full or half empty but completely full at all times, and any other state is an illusion.

10. Try to associate with positive like minded people.

This chapter is not the conclusion of any argument for or against the law of attraction, but rather a collection of thoughts to help in one's journey to find truth. You now may have more questions about this subject than you did an hour ago. That's okay if you are closer to the truth. Any deep study of the book of Job will reveal the truth that Job was not causing his circumstances through wrong thinking as much as God wanted to prove the character of Job. Job's friends, in contrast, argued that Job was responsible for the painful agony that he was experiencing and demanded that he seek forgiveness from God before it's too late. The fact that God would not accept a prayer from them (Eliphaz, Bildad, and Zophar) is evidence that their philosophy was incorrect. God has the final say so in all our circumstances regardless of what we think. But that does not excuse us from taking an optimistic view of life. In the past when people have come up to me asking to explain the law of attraction I simply tell them to read six specific books in order as they are given, and then they will know the concept of the law of attraction. These six books are as follows:

1. **A Happy Pocket Full of Money**
   by David Cameron Gikandi
2. **The God in You**
   by Robert Collier
3. **The Law of the Higher Potential**
   by Robert Collier
4. **The Magic Word**

by Robert Collier

5. The Secret of Power

by Robert Collier

6. The Power of Your Subconscious Mind

by Joseph Murphy

Go buy a package of six different colors of highlighters, and as you read these books highlight what impresses you as important. The six colors are for variety; I sometime have several colors on the same page. Start with "A Happy Pocket Full of Money" to prepare your mind for the journey. After reading each book, go back and read just what you have highlighted. Don't be afraid to annotate in the back of the book some of what you have highlighted. For example, in David's book I have written in the back "102 whatever you believe, you can do". So I know that if I turn to page 102 then a subject similar to what I have written down will be found there. I feel confident that the information in these six books will transform any person who reads them provided they implement the information and endeavor to live in harmony with nature. The law of attraction actually can be summed up in one word: "faith".

Is our destiny controlled by our attitude, or is it controlled by supernatural forces beyond our control, or is it a combination of both? We will discuses this in the next chapter.

Chapter Two

Who Controls Our Destiny?

This chapter is related to the last chapter. Some of the deepest secrets in the universe are hidden in plain sight. All it takes is a simple false paradigm to occlude the most precious truth. We have all seen puzzle mazes. You start in one corner in try to find a path to the center. Oftentimes I would start in the center and work outward. My friends called that cheating, I would call it reverse engineering. When solving the mysteries of the universe we have to be willing to think in reverse as well as forward. We can actually examine the lives of individuals and see evidence of supernatural intervention. Many times a painful or terrible event marks the turning point toward a life of purpose.

Take Professor Dumbledore in the first two Harry Potter movies for example: That character was played by Richard Harris. I have always thought of Richard as an actor, but he was not always an actor. Acting was not Richard's first love; rugby was. Richard's love and skill of the game was so pronounced that he was destined to become a professional rugby player until something terrible happened. While still in his teens Richard mysteriously contracted tuberculosis and was too ill to ever compete in rugby again, but not so ill as to not act. In fact Richard only considered attending acting school only after failing to find proper training in the art of directing. It was only after the rugby and film directing doors had been painfully closed that he considered acting as a profession. Perhaps we can look in our own lives and see where an event has given direction. I do not believe that such events are happenstance. Let us now examine the lives of others whose experience bear the marks of divine guidance.

The lives of Charles Kettering, Henry Leland, Ralph Budd, and others are but a few of the examples in history of individuals whose destiny was shaped by providence and faith.

Charles Kettering

By our standards Charles Kettering's early life was one scarred by poverty, but he didn't seem to notice. He never complained about the present condition, he only looked forward to the future. As a child he had spent many hours barefoot behind a plough. He liked working with his hands. He would dismantle his mother's sewing machine, unwind the coils and rewind them on the bobbin winder. Little did he know where that habit would lead to. After graduating high school in the summer of 1895, Charles was hired as a school teacher at a nearby school. He taught first at a small school named Bunker Hill and later at a larger school in Mifflin. Charles's parents wanted him to be a minister so during the summer of 1896 he took Greek at the College of Wooster in Wooster Ohio. While studying Greek at Wooster Charles just happen to find a catalogue of Ohio State University. He noticed that the curriculum of engineering courses included blacksmithing. He didn't know what engineering was, but he knew he could save some money if could make his own horseshoes. He also had a painful bought of severe headaches brought on partially from his failing eyesight. This was a reoccurring condition. In the summer of 1897, after teaching for only one semester at Mifflin, Charles Kettering was made principal of the school. This happened as a result of the unexpected resignation of then principal Neil McLaughlin, a former teacher of Charles'. After completing his second year of teaching at Mifflin, Charles eyesight improved. This prompted him to enroll at Ohio State University in the fall of 1898. By the third trimester of his freshman year his eyesight and headaches were so intense that he was unable to read, and his roommates had to read all his homework to him. Charles started his sophomore year only to quit college because of his severe headaches. He was devastated. He thought all his hopes and dreams had come to an end. He didn't understand why God had allowed tragedy to rob him of his dreams. The truth is that this tragedy would bring him the life of his dreams. Charles accepted his fate and decided to travel back home to see what else God had in store for him. **It just so happened** that as Charles was in Mifflin visiting some of his friends that the telephone company was in town setting telephone poles for a new line. Charles thought that fresh air and physical labor would improve his medical condition, so he signed up and was hired on. Charles began digging holes for telephone poles, and soon became the foreman of the crew. Not long after this Charles was asked to install telephone line exchanges. Charles didn't know the first thing about line exchanges, but he saw this as an opportunity not an obstacle. **Coincidentally** a book entitled "American Telephone Practice" had just been published detailing everything a person needs to know about line exchanges, so he sent for it. As part of installing line exchanges Charles had to match the resistance inside the exchange with that on the outside of the exchange. He calculated the values needed for the relays and impedance coils, but there was just one problem. The relays and coils with those values didn't exist! The exact relays and impedance coils he needed had never been made before. So he then did what he had done so many times on his mother's sewing machine. He dismantled and rewound the impedance coils to match the values he needed, and he did it on a bobbin winder of an old sewing machine. In time he was entrusted with greater responsibility and more complex tasks. Charles Kettering became a real asset to the telephone company, and in return Charles gained valuable experience. Charles' eyesight improved while working for the telephone company, so in the fall of 1901 after about two years of manual labor he decided to start his sophomore year for the second time at Ohio State University. Once again poor eyesight and severe headaches hindered his education, but fortunately Charles had two wonderful roommates at the boarding house he stayed in, and they read all the necessary home work to Charles. What a coincidence, loving, caring, and helpful friends always seemed to show up at the opportune moments in Charles Kettering's life. Despite his disability Charles had a **positive outlook on life** in general, and he achieved an excellent grade point average. In fact **it just so happened** that during his senior year the professor of physics at the university, A. D. Cole, received a letter from the assistant general manager of the National Cash Register Company (NCR), Mr. Edward A. Deeds requesting a graduating student with an inventive mind and practical experience in electricity. Alfred Cole could think of no one else than Charles Kettering as a prospect for Mr. Deeds. The two years of manual labor with the telephone company proved to be a blessing beyond belief. You see Charles wasn't just hired by NCR; he was hired at a wage more than four times that of an engineering apprentice just graduating college! Charles began working for NCR in July of 1904. Within a few months Charles had invented the OK Charge Phone. He had done this by combining a telephone with a cash register. This was done so that clients could handle credit sales. No other inventor at NCR had done this because they did not have practical experience in the telephone field like Charles had. In August of 1905 Charles married Olive Williams. Olive was a real blessing to Charles for she was astute at home economics and finances; something he didn't care to bother with. She started right away saving for retirement. **It just so happened** that Mr. Deeds had a secretary by the name of Earl Howard who after a short while left NCR to work at the Cadillac Motor Car Company. It wasn't long before Earl was assistant sales manager of the company. After about four years at Cadillac Earl came down to Dayton to visit with old friends and to purpose a problem to Mr. Kettering about the defunct ignition system of Cadillac cars. In those days they used a magneto coupled to a dry cell battery to ignite a continuous shower of sparks in the combustion chambers. The dry cell batteries used did not last long under these conditions, and the cars stalled at low rpm. You were lucky to go more than two hundred miles without having to change batteries. What Charles came up with to solve the problem was the addition of a simple coil wired into the ignition circuit, but he called it an ignition relay switch. This changed the shower of sparks into a single specific timed spark which in turn prolonged the life of the batteries by tenfold! The ignition was more stable too with less misfires and stalling. To accomplish this feat Charles set up a laboratory in a barn at the back Mr. Deed's house. They made the parts they needed in the hay loft and used them on a Cadillac that had been parked down below. Charles made a lot of trips up and down the winding staircase in that old barn. At the onset of the project it became apparent that a milling machine and a lathe was needed to make the parts, and that these machines alone would cost fifteen hundred dollars. It just so happened that Olive had saved up a little more than fifteen hundred dollars in their retirement savings and that the ignition problem that her husband was working on could only be solved by her **letting go** of their savings which was a lot of money in those days. It seems that both Olive and

Charles had a habit of letting go of things rather easily. Letting go is easy to do **when you have confidence that the future will always bring to you just what you need**. After finding a solution to the ignition problem Edward Deeds wrote Henry Leland, the president of Cadillac, a letter informing him on the success of the project. Mr. Leland in turn sent his chief engineer down to inspect the device and test drive a car to assess its operation and report back to Henry. Apparently Fortunes begin to move swiftly for Charles because Henry had called Mr. Kettering and Mr. Deeds to his office in Detroit to award them an unexpected contract to manufacture eight thousand ignition relays. Charles then tried to explain that they were inventers, not manufactures; but Henry would have no part of it, his mind was made up. Both Edward and Charles thought it would take a miracle to pull this one off. It was a challenge to make one device, only a large manufacturing facility could make eight thousand of them. That is when providence came to the rescue. You see, years before when Charles worked at digging holes for telephone poles, and installing telephone line exchanges he became acquainted with Mr. J. B. Edwards, the president of the Kellogg Switchboard and Supply Company in Chicago. Upon finding out of their dire need Mr. Edwards heartily agreed to make all eight thousand ignition sets in one of his factories. It was about this time that Charles

Kettering resigned from NCR to devote all his time to his new calling: improving the automobile ignition system. It was the summer of 1909.

Henry Martyn Leland

Henry Leland was born in 1843 to a farming family in Barton Vermont. In the summer of 1860, while still a teenager, Henry became an apprentice machinist. During the civil war he was kept busy making gun barrels and fabricating rifles for the union army at the Springfield Armory. Henry turned twenty one in 1864. That was an election year and since Henry was just old enough to vote he voted for, and very much admired Abraham Lincoln. In 1872 Henry begin working for Brown & Sharpe, or B & S as some call it, makers of precision measuring instruments. It was during his tenure at Brown & Sharpe that Henry developed his skill as a master precision machinist. This would play a vital role in his future and ours too. During his last few years at B & S he traveled the country doing field work and servicing items made by Brown & Sharpe. It was during this time of his life he happened to run into a man by the name of George Westinghouse. Now George had invented the air brake system for railcars, and was having a lot of problems with the design of his newest brake system. Much to his delight, Henry Leland showed him how his problems could be solved through the principles of precision machining, and subsequently the problem was solved. In 1886 Henry set out to start his own machine shop in Chicago because he thought it would be a profitable city to do business in. He arrived in Chicago on May 4th, the same day the notorious labor riots broke out in the Haymarket square. The police were being bombed and the whole city was in an uproar. The atmosphere here was totally intolerable to any kind of business and the only safe action to take was to leave immediately so Henry headed north. The first place he came to was Detroit. He had already travelled some and knew that Detroit might be a good place to start a business. After locating in Detroit Henry set up a small machine shop, and quickly developed a good reputation as an excellent machinist. There was a store there not far from Henry's shop that sold tools and hardware of the machine shop trade. The owner's name was Charles Strelinger. It wasn't long before Henry and Charles were good friends. Henry was unsatisfied with a small machine shop business. He wanted a large factory, and that took money that he didn't have. It just chance to happen that Charles Strelinger had a friend up in Alpena by the name of Robert Faulconer. Robert had made a lot of money in the lumber business and was looking for something else to invest in. After a detailed meeting a decision was made to form a new machine shop company with Leland as president, Faulconer as vice president. Henry then brought in an old acquaintance from Brown and Sharp by the name of Charles Norton to be head of the tool design department, and Charles Strelinger came on as secretary. The new company was called Leland, Faulconer, and Norton Co. or L, F&N as it was commonly referred to. About this same time Wilfred Leland, Henry's son, was in medical school studying to be a physician. Henry sent for Wilfred and told him that a career as a machinist would be much more profitable in the end than a career as a medical doctor, and then arranged for Wilfred to have apprenticeship training at Brown and Sharpe. After completing his training as an apprentice machinist Wilfred came back to Detroit to work with his father, but ended up selling woodworking trimmers that his father made in his shop for the American Machinery Company. Wilfred was a people person. He had the charm and charisma necessary to make him a top notch salesman. His father on the other hand was factual, meticulous; and sometimes harsh and exacting. In short Henry was rough, Wilfred was smooth. The recession of 1895-1896 stifled the trimmer business and so the Lelands decided to take advantage of the bicycle craze of the 1890's. At that time women loved to ride bicycles and there were not enough machine shops around willing to make gears and sprockets for bicycles. Norton wanted to leave the company to pursue other interest so in 1894 Henry bought out Norton's share of the company, and the name of the company changed to Leland & Faulconer. In 1899 an automotive entrepreneur by the name of Ransom Olds was starting his own car company, and was having trouble making gears for transmissions. Ransom lacked the precision machining talent to perform this type of work and so approached Henry Leland with an offer to make gears. Leland & Faulconer had a reputation for being the best machine shop in the northeast not to mention the extensive experience in the manufacture of bicycle gears. Henry was reluctant to enter the automotive business as this was not his intention, but finally agreed to make transmissions for olds. The name of Ransom's new company's was Olds Motor Works, and it was financed by Mr. Samuel Smith. During the year 1900 Ransom was busy making prototype automobiles to be tested and evaluated to decide which to mass produce. There were eleven models in all, and some were low end, some were middle class and some were high end automobiles. As fate would have it an accidental fire on March, 9th 1901 set by an employee on the engine assembly line destroyed all engine making capabilities as well as all but one prototype car. It was the low end model parked by the front door that survived because it was the only one light enough to be pushed outside to safety. Ransom wasted no time in self pity or negative thinking. He immediately put this model into production calling it the Curved Dash Model, but others called it the Oldsmobile. He also contacted the major machine shops in the area to manufacture the engines for car and Leland & Faulconer was the first he called. The second machine shop he called was one operated two brothers named John and Horace Dodge (The Dodge Brothers), and still others were called. All machine shops were given identical plans to build engines with; but when compared side by side the Dodge brother's engine was 3 horsepower and the Leland & Faulconer engine was 3.7 horsepower. The difference was in precision machining. Again Henry Leland voiced his objection to involvement in the automotive industry, but later relented. Despite the fire, Olds Motor Works still sold about 600 models in 1901 making it the first mass produced low cost automobile in America. In fact Henry Ford use to come to the Olds factory and watch them build cars using what was then called progressive production. Today we know it as mass production or assembly line production. A few years later when Henry Ford started what was to be called the Ford Motor Company, he implemented progressive production and became famous for it because he was much more proficient at it than any one else at that time. Leland & Faulconer was now making the *engine, transmission, and drive gears* for olds. It was in the month of June (1901) that the engineers at Leland & Faulconer found that they could triple the power output just by redesigning the valve ports and raising the compression ratio. Henry gave his approval to build several prototypes to see if it would work. It worked so well he called the redesigned engine "Little Hercules", and enthusiastically informed the plant manager that for a very small investment of time and tooling an engine with three times the horsepower could be produced. The impatient manager then informed Henry that there would be no more delays in production, and that what they had **was good enough**. Henry was visibly upset over the foolishness of an obvious **missed opportunity**. Now he regretted his involvement in the automotive industry.

Henry installed one of the new engines in an Oldsmobile he drove and kept another one in the car for show. It was while contemplating a way out of the automotive business that Henry was contacted by a couple of investors about a failed automotive venture. William Murphy and Lemuel Bowen ask Henry Leland to appraise an automotive business that had failed. They choose Henry because of his experience as an accomplished machinist, and as a person familiar with the automotive industry. When Henry saw the potential of the factory to be liquidated he brought up the option of reorganization to the investors. Murphy and Bowen had never considered it because it was common practice in those days to always sell and accept the loss. Besides, the factory was missing three crucial systems to make a complete car: the *engine, the transmission, and the drive gears.* What a coincidence! Can you imagine the look on Henry's face when he found out that the only items stopping plant production just happen to be items he could ether had in possession, or could readily manufacture? Can you imagine the look on Bill Murphy's face when Henry walked over to his car pulled out a single cylinder engine and said "This is Little Hercules and it can beat any Oldsmobile on the road"? Right there and then the investors decided to reorganize into a new car company provided that Henry Leland come on as operational director of the company. The investors suggested to Henry that the company be named after him like "The Leland Motor Company", but Henry would not have it. The notion of ego entering the business was offensive to the humble nature of Henry Leland. Henry named the company after the French explorer that founded the city of Detroit: Antoine de la Mothe, Sieur de Cadillac. The name of the new company was the Cadillac Automobile Company. It was the end of August 1902. When Henry asked about the former name of the company Murphy replied that it was called the Henry Ford Company, and despite this being his second failed attempt at automobile manufacture, Henry Ford still did not have enough sense to give up making cars. It is as if persistence pays off. By the way, where did Henry ford get his machine shop experience? At the James Flower & Brothers Machine Shop.

Who else worked at the same machine shop? It was David Dunbar Buick. David started out making plumbing fixtures eventually owning half-share in a large and profitable plumbing fixture business. David sold his half of the company for $100,000 to start his own automotive company in January of 1900. Over the next year and a half or so David started and failed in the automotive business three times. In fact David started and failed in the automotive business his whole life, but **he never gave up**. Was his life a waste? Have you ever taken a bath in a porcelain lined bathtub? David was the inventor who discovered a way to bind porcelain to cast iron. It was David Buick and Walter Marr that came up with the overhead valve design of all modern automobile engines! David died without the inspiring knowledge of the thousands of Americans who would drive a car with his name on it, or who would benefit from some of his many inventions and patents (such as the lawn sprinkler). We are better off because he was not a quitter.

During the next three years (1903-1906) over twelve thousand Cadillac's were sold which meant that Cadillac was the best selling car in America. It was during this time period that Cadillac bought out

Robert Faulconer's share of Leland & Faulconer and the two companies combined to form the Cadillac Motor Car Company. Henry Leland now found himself fully invested in the automotive business seeing this was his full time job, and he was also the minority shareholder of Cadillac. Henry Leland also did something to the automotive industry that all other said could not be done, he standardized all part measurements and manufacture. That is all the same parts on Cadillac automobiles were so identical that they were completely interchangeable. A part on one car will always fit on another of the same kind.

The Stanley's

Now our story takes a strange detour to Lewiston Maine where twin brothers operated a photography studio during the 1880s. Francis and Freelan Stanley were inventors, and artists who had helped pioneer the photographic industry. Frances invented the atomizer in 1876 so he could mist water color paints onto his canvas. This invention was the forerunner of the modern airbrush. In 1883 Frances invented a certain dry plate process for photography, and together with his brother Freelan founded the lucrative Stanley Dry Plate Company, the largest manufacturer of photographic plates in New England. Something strange started to happen to Frances in the mid to late

1890s; he became obsessed with steam engines and the horseless carriage industry. In 1897 he built his first steam car just for the fun of it. Less than a year later due to the publicity of their project, the Stanley's were invited to show off their project at Boston's first ever car show. A race was held, and the Stanley car won at a top speed of 27 mph. The Stanley's were then overwhelmed with orders for the car despite the fact they were just having fun and had not considered being a major automobile manufacturer. Over the next two years they made and sold over 200 cars, and that gave them the title of the largest automobile manufacturer in the United States at that time. No sooner than the Stanley's started making cars a man by the name of John Walker came up and offered to buy the business. The Stanley's didn't want to sell, but John offered them a quarter of a million dollars which was such a good deal that they could not refuse. The business was sold in 1899. For the next two years Francis and Freelan were again in the photography business; but there was still a **calling deep in their souls** for something to do with automobiles. For two years they thought about their **obsession** in the automotive industry with an **attitude of faith and expectancy** knowing that some day their dreams would come to true. What happened next was nothing short of a miracle. In 1902 they were given an offer to buy back the company they had sold for only twenty thousand dollars. Not only that, their senior competitor in the photography business just showed up and offered them a fortune for their photography business which they gladly accepted. It is interesting to note that this certain competitor had the **faith, persistence, and insight** to change the world for the better. This competitor was as determined to be as much as a success in the photography business as the Stanley's was in their business. He was George Eastman of Kodak. The Stanley's now have a prosperous automobile company, and the capital to expand the business. The name of their new business was called the Stanley Motor Carriage Company. In 1905 the Royal Automobile Club of England instituted the Dewar Trophy Award to be awarded for the most outstanding achievement in the automotive industry. The Stanley's won this most prestigious award in 1906 for setting the land speed record of 127 mph. in the Stanley Steamer. In 1903, at the age of 53, Freelan Stanley was diagnosed with terminal tuberculosis, and given six months to a year to live. Freelan rededicated his life to be one of optimism, open-mindedness, and a **positive mental attitude**. He also moved to a mountainous region of Colorado where he could bask in the splendor of its beauty. The result of such a change was that Freelan lived to be 91 years old, and that he also built the most opulent hotel in the region at that time. The Stanley Hotel in Estes Park opened on Independence Day in 1909. The

Stanley Hotel has been host to presidents, celebrities, and dignitaries for over one hundred years. Also if you have ever traveled to the Estes Park Fairgrounds, Stanley Park, or Rocky Mountain National Park you might want to thank Freelan Stanley for he was the father of these as well. As fate would have it all of these would not exist if Freelan had not contracted tuberculosis. Tuberculosis was the seed of adversity that blossomed into a blessing for all.

The high quality of Cadillac cars attracted the attention of the Royal Automobile Club of England. In 1908 they had eight models shipped to England three of which were completely disassembled and reassembled after thoroughly mixing up the parts. This was to test the theory of part interchangeability which was believed impossible in those days. The three cars were then driven 500 miles at full throttle to see if they would hold up to standards. The results were so impressive that Cadillac won the Dewar Trophy in 1908. Henry Leland proved to the world that the belief that machined parts could not be made to so close tolerances as to be interchangeable was a lie. Dispelling this false paradigm not only launched the modern automotive industry, but the space industry as well. Cadillac had received so much positive attention in 1908- 1909 that a man by the name of William Durant bought Cadillac for 4.75 million to add to his new automotive conglomerate named

General Motors. Henry Leland wanted to improve the automotive industry; Durant just wanted to control it. William Durant was a massive risk taker though. Mr. Durant asked Henry and Wilfred to stay on to manage Cadillac and to insure stability. During the early years of Cadillac Henry's desire for a self starting automotive engine was so pronounced that he even wrote to the brightest professors in our most prestigious universities for an answer. They all wrote back with the same answer: It was impossible and impractical. This problem was in the mind of Henry for many years. The icy winter of 1910 changed everything. That winter a woman was driving her Cadillac across the Belle Island Bridge when her car stopped right in the middle of the bridge. She was not strong enough to start it herself so she waited for help. Not much later a good friend of Henry Leland, a Mr. Byron Carter drove by in his Cadillac and stopped to help. While Byron was hand cranking the engine the car backfired resulting in an immediate broken arm and jaw. Byron was laid out unconscious and bleeding on the bridge. A few minutes later a couple of Cadillac engineers by the names of Earnest and William drove up and stopped to help, started the woman's car, and rushed Byron to the hospital where he later died of complications of his injuries. Henry was devastated. Every year hundreds of people are injured or killed by hand starting their vehicles, and

Henry was determined to not one more person would die attempting to start a Cadillac. In desperation he called up Charles Kettering to ask him if the remotest possibility even existed that this problem could be solved. Charles gave him an answer that he had not heard before. Charles enthusiastically proclaimed that all things were possible and encouraged Henry to not worry about it. Charles put all of his mind and body into helping his friend Henry out. Charles and Henry had at least one thing in common: They loved people and used money. William Durant loved money and used people. Charles and Edward Deeds worked around the clock in the barn loft winding copper wire on stators like winding thread on a bobbin until they had a small motor with enough torque to start an engine. On February 17, 1911 they had a working model installed on a Cadillac parked down below. Henry Leland was immediately called and informed of the progress so that plans could be made for the manufacture of a self starting Cadillac. The desires of Henry Leland came to fruition because he had the **persistence, emotion, and faith** to materialize his thoughts. The 1912 Cadillac was the first self starting automobile in America. By 1920 most cars on the road were self starting.

In 1913 Cadillac won the prestigious Dewar trophy for the second time for the introduction to the self starting automobile. This is not an annual award, but a trophy awarded only on occasions of exceptional automotive excellence. In the hundred years since the Stanley's won it in 1906 it has been given out only about forty times.

Henry and Wilfred introduced the V-8 engine design into the 1914 Cadillac with much success. By 1915 William Durant had bought enough stock to take over General Motors and become its president. He was expelled in 1910 by the bankers and the board of directors for a reckless and controlling attitude. It was Durant's obsession that he control General Motors, and he had the **persistence, faith, and determination** to do it. Durant and Leland were always in disagreement on issues of humanity and money. To Durant money came first. To Leland people came first. Leland fought for the advancement of the automotive industry and others. Durant fought for the advancement of himself. When World War 1 began, Henry Leland had strong emotional feelings about it. He had traveled in Europe several times, and had friends there. Henry was determined to help his friends in England so he confronted Billy Durant on the conversion of the General Motors plant into and aircraft engine plant. Durant wouldn't allow it on the basis of lost profits. After conferring with his family, Henry and Wilfred decided to take immediate action by resigning from and leaving Cadillac (letting go) and forming a new company to make aircraft engines for the United States Army Air Core. With funding from the government Henry set out at the age of 74 to help his friends in Europe by building the liberty aircraft engine to power the dh-4 aircraft. He named the new company after his favorite president, Lincoln. After the war ended Henry once again found himself without a job, so with a little help from investors the Lincoln Motor Company was retooled for automotive use, and in 1920 the first Lincoln Model L rolled off the assembly line. Despite the fact that the Lincoln luxury car was the major competitor of the Cadillac luxury car, sales were slow. The Company became insolvent, and in 1922 was bought by Henry Ford at an auction for eight million dollars. Henry Leland was the father of the two car companies devoted to a higher standard of living, and he achieved his success the same way all others before or since him have: through **faith, persistence and focusing his thoughts on what he desired** instead of the apparent obstacles in his path.

Edward Budd

Edward G. Budd was born in Delaware in 1870. At the age of 17 he started out as a machinist apprentice in Philadelphia. In 1899 Ed went to work at the American Pulley Company where he learned the steel fabrication industry. At that time all automobiles were made of wood, but Edward believed that steel would be a far superior material to wood in the manufacture of car bodies. Unfortunately most people accepted the status quo of wood car bodies but not Edward. He was determined to find a cost effective way to make steel car bodies despite being told that it was impossible. He then worked at the Hale & Kilburn Manufacturing Company where he learned a new kind of fabricating steel called pressed steel. The pressed steel technique was used to make steel hubs for railroad cars. Edward then entered the automotive industry in 1912 building steel bodies for automobiles using the same technology he used to make steel hubs. His company was called the Budd Company and it catered to many foreign car manufacturers. In 1916 the Dodge brothers decided that steel was the way to go and so began the process of making every Dodge with a steel body. This was a considered a **risky** maneuver by many in the business, but it paid off. Customers recognized the added quality of Dodge vehicles and flocked to buy one. As a result Dodge sold its millionth car in 1923! When the great depression hit the automotive business suffered, and that caused Edward Budd to do something different. Like Henry Leland he decided to focus on improvement and **giving** instead of self pity and **getting**. Edward decided to experiment with a new type of steel called 18-8. The 18 stood for eighteen percent chromium and the 8 for eight percent nickel making this steel what we call today stainless steel. Many at the time gave up on using stainless steel because it could not be welded by common means without warping, and damaging the rust prevention properties of the steel. That didn't stop Edward from his dreams, for out of the combination of Edward Budd's **positive mental attitude** and the **open minded attitude** of his associate Earl Ragsdale was born the invention of the "shotwelding" process of stainless steel fabrication which preserved all the strength and characteristics of the steel. Even though the Budd Company manufactured most of the steel automobile bodies in the United States; Edward set his thoughts on something larger: Railcars.

Ralph Budd

Ralph Budd was born into a poor farming community in 1879. In 1898 he began working as a draftsman for the Chicago Great Western Railway's engineering department. In 1902 he began working for the Chicago, Rock Island and Pacific Railroad under the supervision of John Stevens. John had already proven himself a successful and capable engineer, so when President Theodore Roosevelt choose an engineer to build the Panama Canal; he choose John Stevens to head up the project. John saw the attributes of **faith** and **open-mindedness** in Ralph and so choose Ralph to be his aid and helper in everything he did. In 1910 John and Ralph moved to Oregon to work together on the Great Northern Railway. Their boss was James J. Hill the founder of the Great Northern Railway. James had a nickname of "The Empire Builder". Most of the railways built in the northwest were built by James Hill. James had a vision of a transcontinental railway, but others in the industry said it was an impossible feat to consider. James surrounded himself with successful people, and he saw leadership and success written all over Ralph Budd. In fact James Hill confided with John Stevens that upon his passing that Ralph should be made president of the railway. And that is exactly what happened. In 1919 at the age of 40 Ralph Budd became the youngest president of any railway in the United States. Ralph loved people and used money so the first project Ralph embarked on was based on his love for humanity. The great railway avalanche of 1910 in Wellington Washington still stands as the worst avalanche accident in American history. With this catastrophe still fresh in the minds of most Americans; Ralph set out to make sure this would never happen again by doing something most considered impossible. A railway tunnel nearly eight miles long would have to be built through a mountain of solid rock. The Cascade Tunnel that Ralph started in Washington was completed in 1929 and still today remains the longest railway tunnel in the United States at 7.79

miles long. The stock market crash of 1929 brought changes in the rail industry. Passenger traffic slowed to a near halt as the depression deepened. Ralph Budd knew what the railroad needed but ran into stiff resistance from others in the business because they were **afraid of the unknown** and **afraid of change**. Ralph embarked on an ambitious plan to revitalize the rail industry. In 1932 Ralph left the Great Northern Railway to be president of the Chicago, Burlington and Quincy Railroad. The Burlington as it was also called had better scenery along its routes and this was part of Budd's plans to increase passenger revenue. In the midst of the great depression while others were planning for hard times; Ralph Budd was planning for prosperity. Budd envisioned a passenger car so sleek and modern looking that only a science fiction comic book could entertain the idea. While looking for materials to build a train that looked more like a rocket; he ran into Edward Budd at an auto show. Edward was showing off new car bodies made of space age looking stainless steel. Ralph inquired about the physical properties of stainless steel to decide whether or not it would be suitable for rail transport. The answer he received from Edward inspired him with hope. In Edwards opinion there was no better material to build trains from. Ralph and Edward immediately began building the most advanced passenger train in existence. This was accomplished despite the fact that they did not have an engine for it. The only engines available for trains at that time were steam and gas electric. Nether had the long distance capabilities needed to make the transcontinental trip needed for a true sightseeing adventure. Ralph knew that only a diesel engine could do what he envisioned, but they were too large and heavy to even consider. Diesel engines in the 1920s were as big as a small house and used mostly for large passenger ships, cargo ships, or power plants. The name of the new class of streamlined trains was Zephyr. The first one was completed in time to show off at the 1933 worlds fair in Chicago. Ralph had stepped out in faith believing God would work some sort of miracle that would enable him to travel long distances without stopping for fuel or water. An engine that could do this and still have the horse power to pull a train up a steep grade was just not in existence. Ralph needed a miracle, and he needed to get this problem off his mind so he walked around the fair looking at the various exhibits. He found the automotive exhibits particularly interesting.

The 1933 World's Fair

The 1933 World's fair is a miracle in of itself. It was one of the most popular and most attended world's fairs ever in history. Although the fair was scheduled to close in November; the popularity of the event would not allow the fair to close until October of 1934! The motto of the fair was "**A century of progress**". This was in stark contrast to the dark times of the depression they were in. Despite the depression this fair accomplished something no other fair had done; the bond holders were completely paid up by the time the fair ended in 1934. The fair was started by a nonprofit corporation in 1928 and it was at this time they applied for a ten million dollar bond to finance the fair. Some people say that it was just coincidence, and still others say it was supernatural intervention, but the bond was issued on October 28th 1929. Just a few hours after having the bond in hand the stock market crashed ending any future possibility of funding for the fair. The fair was a miracle in the making. The fair organizers envisioned an assembly line in the main automotive exhibit. Only the Ford Motor Company was considered for this exhibit because Henry Ford pioneered the mass manufacture of automobiles. But something strange happened when the idea was brought before Ford. Henry Ford **procrastinated** on the decision and plans for this exhibit. Over time the fair planning committee decided to make the same offer to General Motors. Immediately a man with **definiteness of purpose** saw an opportunity and acted. That man was William Knudson, the president of a new division of General Motors called Chevrolet. William had worked for the Ford Motor Company from 1911 to 1921 so he was an experienced at assembly line design and set up. Is it just a coincidence that Bill Knudson was working for Ford and General Motors at the infancy of the most modern breakthroughs in the assembly line manufacturing? No one was more qualified to build the exhibit than he. William Knudson was so **motivated and focused** on this exhibit that he funded half of it himself. As plans for the exhibit progressed an apparent insurmountable problem emerged with the power supply. The assembly line itself needed a thousand horsepower engine to pull the weight of chain and automobiles along the assembly line. A diesel engine would work well but they were too large to transport. When all hope seemed to drain out of the project an open mind came to the rescue. Someone had brought the problem to the head of General Motors research division, Charles Kettering, with the word impossible. You just don't walk in and say impossible to Charles Kettering. Charles immediately obtained blueprints for a large diesel engine, looked them over and allowed his subconscious to work out the details over time. Actually Charles had been toying around with diesel engine design since 1921 but had no real reason to get serious about it. After a tour in Europe to examine their diesel engine factories, he decided a radical change was needed to solve the problem. He then redesigned the engine from a four stroke to a two stroke engine which not only made the engine smaller but also increased the power of the engines. The Winton Engine Company made the two new engines to specs as Charles had requested. Without knowing if the engines would run the two prototypes were crated and shipped to the exhibit site at the worlds fair. This was due to the tight schedule of the fair. The engines did each run at six hundred horsepower to power the assembly line, but not without problems. The problems were fixed along the way and the exhibit was an astounding success.

Ralph Budd attended the General Motors exhibit to divert his mind from business. A calm spirit came over him as he watched Chevrolet cars roll down the assembly line. It was as if God was telling him not to worry. That dreams really do come true. At the end of the exhibit something caught his eye which caused him to rub his face in disbelief. He asked a tall, lanky man nearby to explain what these was, and tears welled up in his eyes as Charles Kettering described the new small, two stroke diesel engines which had just been brought into existence. The new eight cylinder engine had plenty of power to take any train up the steepest grade, and was just the right size to fit the new zephyr passenger train. Ralph ordered an engine for the Zephyr. The new improved engine was delivered in the early spring of 1934 and on May 26 a test run was made from Denver to Chicago. The thousand mile trip took just over thirteen hours which made this the fastest train in the United States. On a straight stretch of track the train got up to 112.5 miles per hour. This was when the present land speed record was 115 miles per hour! Out of Kettering's new design of diesel engine came the twelve and sixteen cylinder engines that powered our first diesel submarines. Charles Kettering was a man who mixed **faith** with **creative imagination**. The 1933 world's fair showed the world the true traits of leadership in William Knudson. At the start of World War 2 President Roosevelt ordered a commission of Lieutenant General for William. This was the highest initial rank ever bestowed upon a civilian. It is not luck that propels people to the highest levels of success. It is specific traits of character, an optimistic perception of our environment, and a firm belief that nothing is impossible.

A Work of Art

Throughout his entire life Henry Leland has always aimed for the highest standards in his personal as well as business life. He also has always expected the same from others. Unfortunately Henry has also experienced the pain of persecution that awaits those whose work bears the stamp of genius. Society encourages mediocrity. I have always read Foxe's Book of Martyrs through the eyes of a theologian, but this is a book as much on society as religion. We have to accept the fact that publically burning people to death ceased because society had changed. But human nature is still the same. Whether it's Henry Leland, Tesla, or Copernicus, successful people draws criticism like a lightning rod draws lightning. Henry's high standards set him apart like a lonely tree on a hilltop in a thunder storm. It seems that everywhere he went he was criticized unduly. Why is it that society applauds a barely get by mentality and then offers resistance to those who go the extra mile? This is what Henry Leland wanted to know. Henry became fed up and had decided to vent his frustration to the public. He did have the wisdom to hire a man by the name of Theodore MacManus to write the reproof. It was published under the title "The Penalty of Leadership" in the January 2nd 1915 issue of The Saturday Evening Post. Today it is still regarded as a work of art in the field of literacy. If Henry had written it himself it would have been tainted with the venom of bitter emotions. When I had recently read the article I noticed how the word 'follower' was used: "Failing to equal or excel, the follower seeks to depreciate and to destroy—but only confirms once more the superiority of that which he strives to supplant." Truly this was a masterpiece of literacy for the word follower is used in the exact same context as the word drifter in Napoleon hill's book titled "Outwitting the Devil". In fact Napoleon hill discusses drifting more than any other single subject in the book. It was the drifters in life that criticized Leland, Tesla and others. Drifters or followers of society feel comfortable in mediocrity. They see successful people as boat rockers or people that may cause change. Change brings with it the unknown. Fear of change and fear of the unknown are only problems to those who have no faith. Henry Leland had faith, leadership abilities, and was a master-machinist and a master of his own life. With that I leave you a quote from the Penalty of Leadership. "Master-poet, master-painter, master-workman, each in his turn is assailed, and each holds his laurels through the ages"

Summary

The people you have just read about were successful because of the choices they made. In faith they stepped out onto the race of life with hope and definiteness of purpose. They listen to intuition and ignored the drifting masses. The power of choice was their friend and strength of character was their badge of honor. Their living example is evidence that the intangible attributes that God offers freely to us all can catapult us to the highest levels of success.

So we come back to the question "Who controls our destiny?" The answer is really very simple. We control half and God controls half. God builds the race track and we run on it. We have to acknowledge that Charles Kettering's life would have taken a different path if he had good eyesight. And Henry Leland's future would have been vastly different if the Olds factory hadn't burned down in 1901 and if Henry Ford hadn't gone out of business shortly there after. What if Byron Carter hadn't died so prominently in the winter of 1910-1911? Why is it that out of tragedy springs forth blessings that benefit millions? Is it possible that God is waiting for some of us to get off the couch and do our part by living a life of purpose? God has already planned a bright future for us, but we need to make the choice to live that life. God has already done his part. The ball is in our court per say. Our destiny is up to us. We have the power to go in any direction we choose in life. A wise and prudent person will learn from the mistakes and successes of our ancestors. This is why history is recorded. Who controls your destiny? You are responsible for your choices that determine your destiny.

The Race Parable

This is a parable that I tell in all of my seminars to demonstrate a basic truth in self help. The truth is that the glass is nether half empty nor half full, but completely full at all times. The race parable is related to two parables in the bible which we will discuss later. The race parable is a simple visualization exercise.

Imagine that you at the starting line of a race, the race of life. On both sides of you are professional runners much faster than you, not just a few, but many runners. You have all day to win the race, but the finish line is twenty miles away! You know that after running a couple hundred feet that you will be out of breath. You also know that running is a dangerous sport, and that the safest thing for you to do is to stand still and wish for life to be over with. Despair sets in and you decide that it is hopeless to start the race to begin with. From all appearances you have no chance what so ever to win the race.

To many people this is the way life seems. The truth is that we were never told that we had to win any race; we were just told to run in the race. Since we do not live in a competitive universe the notion that there are other runners in the race is a false paradigm. We live in a world of illusion, a giant web of lies designed for one purpose: to make us quit before we even start the race. In reality we do have all day to win the race, but the race track is only eight feet long. There are billions of people on this planet that are standing motionless at the starting line of life waiting for the illusion to change when all they have to do to find success is step out in faith against all they see. This point is so important that Jesus told two parables on it. One parable is found in Matthew 25, and the other in Luke 19. These two parables are best read from the Message version of the Bible. I will be quoting from the Message version when referring to these two parables. Read these for yourself.

In Matthew 25:14-30 we read a parable about a master going on a trip and he leaves money with three of his servants. The first servant gets five thousand, the second servant gets two thousand, and the third servant gets one thousand. All three servants were told what to do with the money. The first two servants doubled their money in a spirit OBEDIENCE and FAITH. The third servant froze out of FEAR and buried the money for safekeeping. One of the first things the third servant told the master when the master came back was "I was afraid". The master replied to the third servant: "That's a terrible way to live! It's criminal to live cautiously like that!" "Take the thousand and give it to the one who risked the most. And get rid of this "play-it-safe" who won't go out on a limb."

Why does God want us to take risks? Because the fears we have in life that keep us from living the life we should live are based on false paradigms. Logically there is never a reason to have fear; this concept is covered in chapter four.

The parable in Luke 19:11-27 is similar to Matthew 25 in that a ruler goes on a long trip. In this parable the ruler gives ten servants money before he leaves on a trip. When he comes back the first servant reports that he doubled the ruler's money, the second servant reports that he made fifty percent profit, and the third servant hid his in a cellar. The third servant told the ruler "I was a little afraid." The ruler replied "Take the money from him and give it to the servant who doubled my stake." "Risk your life and get more than you ever dreamed of. Play it safe and end up holding the bag." Keep in mind that money is not the focus of the parables. If the third servant had stepped out in FAITH and OBEYED the master/ruler and still lost the money on an investment he would still be honorable. It was acting out of FEAR and DOUBT that upset the master, not the loss of money. These parables have more to do with RISK than money. Chapter seven in Bob Proctor's book "You Were Born Rich" is all about taking risk. In that chapter Bob details the fact that wealthy successful people seem to not fear risk. Considering what the Bible has to say about risk, it should be a common topic in church.

Chapter Three

Letting Go

This is one the most important concepts in self-help. The concept of detachment, releasing, or letting go is ubiquitous in the self-help community. Bob Doyle refers to it in his book "Wealth Beyond Reason" (page 44). David Cameron Gikandi talks about it in his book "A Happy Pocket Full of Money" (pages 75, 141, 164, 185). Dr. Wayne Dyer mentions it in his book "Excuses Begone!" (page 113). It is important that Christians become familiar with the concept of letting go because it is emphasized in scripture. I have to note here that the opposite of letting go is ownership, a topic also discussed in self-help books.

I remember as a young adult listening to my grandfather describe in vivid detail the stories of the great depression. He would give first hand accounts of people jumping off of buildings because they were wealthy and had lost everything in the stock market. I would listen to this and wonder how someone could be more emotionally attached to wealth than to their own lives. The truth is that they owned their wealth and their wealth owned them. It was a symbiotic relationship where if one was removed, the other would die. Maybe this is what the Bible refers to as the deceitfulness of riches. The mindset of ownership is dangerous and is to be avoided. We can avoid this trap by cultivating a mindset of letting go. Let us read what the Bible says about letting go.

John 12:24-25 MSG

"Listen carefully: Unless a grain of wheat is buried in the ground, dead to the world, it is never any more than a grain of wheat. But if it is buried, it sprouts and reproduces itself many times over. In the same way, anyone who holds on to life just as it is destroys that life. But if you **let it go**, reckless in your love, you'll have it forever, real and eternal."

Luke 17:33 MSG

"If you grasp and cling to life on your terms, you'll lose it, but if you **let that life go**, you'll get life on God's terms."

Mark 10:17-22 MSG

"As he went out into the street, a man came running up, greeted him with great reverence, and asked, "Good Teacher, what must I do to get eternal life?" 18-19Jesus said, "Why are you calling me good? No one is good, only God. You know the commandments: Don't murder, don't commit adultery, don't steal, don't lie, don't cheat, honor your father and mother." 20He said, "Teacher, I have—from my youth—kept them all!" 21Jesus looked him hard in the eye—and loved him! He said, "There's one thing left: Go sell whatever you own and give it to the poor. All your wealth will then be heavenly wealth. And come follow me." 22The man's face clouded over. This was the last thing he expected to hear, and he walked off with a heavy heart. **He was holding on tight to a lot of things, and not about to let go.**"

Luke 14:26, 33 MSG

"Anyone who comes to me but refuses to **let go** of father, mother, spouse, children, brothers, sisters—yes, even one's own self!—can't be my disciple."

"Simply put, if you're not willing to take what is dearest to you, whether plans or people, and kiss it good-bye, you can't be my disciple."

We see here that letting go is part of salvation. Only by letting go can we attain true wealth and freedom. We cannot hold on to the world with one hand and eternal life with the other. Not long after the wilderness fast, Jesus gave a sermon in his home church. For this the congregation tried to kill him by throwing him off a nearby cliff. One reason for the intense anger from the tithe paying, regular attending church members is Jesus' example of letting go. Jesus told the story of Elijah found in First Kings chapter seventeen. In the story God tells Elijah to go to a woman in Zarephath in Sidon. This is where pagans lived, not Jews. The whole area was in a prolonged famine and many people were starving to death. Upon arriving in Zarephath Elijah asks a woman for water to drink and something to eat. The woman then informs Elijah that all she has is a handful of flour to bake a last meal for her and her son. If all you had was a small pancake to split between you and your child, and a stranger came and ask for it, what would you do? Sometimes it is not easy to let go. Keep in mind that as Jesus was giving the sermon the congregation was well aware of the implication that the reason why Elijah was not sent to Israel was that there was no one there willing to let go. Only a pagan woman in Zarephath was willing to let go. This is why they were so angry. The concept of letting go as described in First Kings is foreign to modern society. If I have ten

Lamborghinis and I gave you one, is that letting go? If all I have is a bicycle and I let you have it, is that letting go? Total unattachment to everything we have or ever will have is total freedom. This is what real letting go is. This is what Jesus preached.

Some years ago Joe Vitale wrote a book titled The Key: the missing secret for attracting anything you want! More than a quarter of the book is about clearing techniques. Simply put clearing techniques are ways to let go. Apparently letting go is something that Joe takes seriously.

Forgiveness is also a form of letting go. The hate, resentment, anger, or vengeance that we have as a result of a past personal event is a burden that can hinder all personal achievement. Christians of all people should be proficient at letting go of the pains of the past through forgiveness. Christians have no excuse for not forgiving others. When I think of forgiveness I think of the story of John Philpot. You can read it for yourself in Foxe's book of Martyrs in the chapter titled The Fires of Smithfield. One of the first things John said to Bishop Gardiner after the bishop pronounced the sentence of death by burning at the stake was "bless you". At supper time on Tuesday the seventeenth (The year was 1555), when a messenger came to inform John the execution was tomorrow, John repaired to his private chambers, and on his knees thanked god that he was worthy to suffer for the truth. Just seconds before the court officers chained him to the stake; John took what money he had on him and divided it amongst the officers! Our forgiveness is not measured by how we treat our friends, but how we treat our enemies.

Matthew 6:12-14 AMP

"Give us this day our daily bread. 12And **forgive us** our debts, as we also have forgiven (left, remitted, and **let go** of the debts, and have given up resentment against) our debtors. 13And lead (bring) us not into temptation, but deliver us from the evil one. For Yours is the kingdom and the power and the glory forever. Amen. 14 For if you **forgive people** their trespasses [their reckless and willful sins, leaving them, **letting them go**, and giving up resentment], your heavenly Father will also forgive you."

The mindset of letting go is a beneficial habit to have.

Chapter Four

Romans 8:28

Romans 8:28 is the central self-help verse in the whole Bible. A proper biblical understanding of self improvement begins with the constant awareness of the concept of Romans 8:28. I will give this verse in several versions so that a fuller understanding of the concept can be achieved.

NKJV

"And we know that all things work together for good to those who love God, to those who are the called according to His purpose."

NIV

"And we know that in all things God works for the good of those who love him, who have been called according to his purpose."

NASB

"And we know that God causes all things to work together for good to those who love God, to those who are called according to His purpose."

MSG (vs.26-28)

"Meanwhile, the moment we get tired in the waiting, God's Spirit is right alongside helping us along. If we don't know how or what to pray, it doesn't matter. He does our praying in and for us, making prayer out of our wordless sighs, our aching groans. He knows us far better than we know ourselves, knows our pregnant condition, and keeps us present before God. That's why we can be so sure that **every detail in our lives of love for God is worked into something good.**"

NCV

"We know that in everything God works for the good of those who love him. They are the people he called, because that was **his plan**."

CEV

"We know that God is always at work for the good of everyone who loves him. They are the ones God has chosen for his purpose"

AMP

"We are assured and know that [God being a partner in their labor] all things work together and are [fitting into a **plan**] for good to and for those who love God and are called according to [His] **design** and purpose."

GW

"We know that all things work together for the good of those who love God—those whom he has called according to his plan."

By now you should be familiar with Romans 8:28. How do we know that we are called according to God's plans and purposes? The fact that you are reading this book is a good sign that you are called, but the verse says that those who love God are called. The truth is that all those who choose the upward path of righteousness in this conflict of good and evil will be given a mission from God. I don't want to get into the subject of predestination, but you will have to accept the fact that you may have been foreordained from the beginning of time to fulfill a special purpose for

God and the good of mankind. God has assured that everything you will ever need to fulfill your mission in life will be provided to you. We have to acknowledge that our existence is a part of God's plan and not an accident.

There are several key benefits that we gain from the understanding of Romans 8:28, the first of which is worry. Romans 8:28 totally negates all worry. All circumstances that you may encounter whether good or evil is measured and calculated by God specifically for your ultimate benefit in self and character improvement. There is nothing to worry about ever. Anything painful or unpleasant that we may encounter is there only for our benefit. From this viewpoint all future events that we may encounter is a positive event. Contemplating this fact alone is a cause for gratitude. This explains why some people express gratitude for a seemingly negative event. When the apostle Peter was to be executed by crucifixion, he was overcome with gratitude and begged to be crucified upside down because he felt unworthy to accept the blessing of dying in the same manner as Jesus. Another example is the reception Paul and Silas received from the town of Philippi. It all began with a fortune telling slave girl who followed Paul and Silas around proclaiming that Paul and Silas were servants of the Most High God. While this may sound good, her annoying attitude gave her away as a woman possessed with an evil spirit.

As soon as Paul recognized this he immediately cast out the demon. This woman was a valuable source of income for her masters by reason of her spirit inspired fortune telling abilities. With the evil spirit gone so was a valuable source of income. This led to hard feelings which in turn led to false accusations which in turn again led to Paul and Silas having their robes ripped off so that they could be beaten many times with a rod before being thrown in to prison and put in stocks. How would you react if this had happened to you? By the time they were secured in prison it was after dark, and late at night. What Paul did next speaks as the level of self improvement he had accomplished. "...about midnight Paul and Silas were praying and singing hymns of praise to God" (NASB). Read the story yourself in Acts chapter sixteen. The jailor that put Paul and Silas in stocks ended up cleaning their wounds where they had been beaten. Not only that, he and his entire household were baptized that night. This story is a good example of Romans 8:28 in action. Eventually all things did work out in concert with God's ultimate plan for the betterment of all parties involved. From this story we learn to always have an attitude of praise and prayer in our lives. Bible scalars have long discussed what Paul was praying about while he was in prison. We just don't know. Some theologians however believe that Paul was expressing the deepest levels of gratitude and forgiveness while he was in stocks with severe wounds on his back. There are other lessons we can learn from this story. First: The person that compliments you could have an evil spirit. Second: The jailor that shackles your feet may be your best friend.

Another benefit of Romans 8:28 is that it pertains to fear. Romans 8:28 totally negates all fear. Some of the most common fears we have are fear of the future, fear of the unknown, fear of change, and fear of failure. Fear of the future is not a concern because we are always living in the now and God has ample ability to resolve any past, present, or future problems we may have in the now. Our fear of the future can nullify our faith in God's ability to help us in the future. Likewise our faith in God's ability to help us in any situation at any time cancels out fear of the future. Regardless of what the future holds, we do not need to be afraid of it. Is not living in the now is a major theme in self help books?

Ecclesiastes 5:20 MSG

"...God deals out joy in the present, the now. It's useless to brood over how long we might live."

Fear of change is somewhat related to fear of the future because of Daniel 12:1. The interpretation most Christians give Daniel 12:1 is that the last generation on earth will have to endure through the worst time of trouble (distress) the world has ever seen. This has caused many Christians to have fear. Without going through the detailed description of this time as described in Matthew 24 and Revelation 6-18; I will simply state that this time period will be a time of great change. Change is like falling down a long flight of stairs. On the way down there is total disorientation, and at the bottom we struggle to get our bearings of up, down, north, south, east, and west. What Daniel 12:1 says is that before we can get our bearings something else happens to cause disorientation. What Romans 8:28 says is that even in the midst of disorientation, we have no reason to worry because all change is going to work toward our ultimate good.

Fear of the unknown is similar to fear of the future. Fear of the unknown is like driving at high speeds on a narrow road at night in fog so dense that you can only see ten feet in front of you. That sounds risky. What kind of risks lay in the realm of the unknown? What kind of rewards lay in the realm of the unknown? Why is it when we were children we looked at the unknown as an adventure, and as adults we see the unknown as a dangerous place full of monsters? Have you ever seen a child open a Christmas present? Children don't know what is in the box, but that doesn't curb their faith and enthusiasm. When adults open a gift, they are not so optimistic. Romans 8:28 assures us that we can travel the unknown at the fastest speeds with the faith and optimistic enthusiasm of a child. We know this for three reasons. One: Life really is an adventure. Two: The unknown is only unknown to us, it is not unknown to the God that charts our course and gives us our mission in life. Three: Because all things known and unknown work together for our good, there are bountiful blessings just waiting for us in the unknown. Considering what the Bible and self help says about the unknown, fear of the unknown is not logical. What if we strike out into the unknown and we fail? That brings us to fear of failure.

The word failure is like the word deserving. They have both been inoculated with the false paradigms of society and slipped into our mental programming like a virus. I've seen people turn down pay raises and work their whole lives at minimum wage because they were told as a child by their parents that they were worthless and undeserving. All humans are equally deserving of pain, pleasure, wealth, or poverty. We can choose whatever path in life we want to take, but we should never avoid a path because we think we are undeserving. I can never be deserving of eternal life, but that doesn't stop me from pursuing it. The same is true with failure. Failure is unduly attached to a negative connotation. One of the false paradigms associated with failure is finality. Failure is not a dead end road; it is part of a process. When babies fall down they don't stay down and dwell on failure, they get back up and forget the past. Unfortunately the negative belief systems of society have had its destructive influence on us adults. We don't see the anomaly of failure for what it really is: a small part of a large process that will always work to our benefit if we let it. Another false paradigm associated with failure is negative emotion. We should never attach negative emotion to what people call failure. If you are new to self-help you might try a neutral or no emotion approach to failure. As we develop and change our thinking correctly toward optimism we can even attach a positive emotion to failure. I can rejoice in my failures because I now see them as evidence of the impending success that is just around the corner. The proper Christian view of failure should be: any accomplishment or failure we can ever have, no matter how large or small will seem so insignificant when Jesus comes that they will actually pass into nonexistence In other words, if it doesn't bother me a million years in the future, I shouldn't worry about it now. From a Christian perspective the only thing that matters is where we are a million years from now. This is why I call failure an anomaly. This is why so many other self-help gurus such as Leo Shriven say that failure doesn't even exist. The meaning and the emotions that society has given failure has turned failure into a false paradigm. In truth failure doesn't exist, only the false idea of it does. The truth is that all things including what we call failure work together for our good and this is Gods plan. Romans 8:28 negates all failures, fears, monsters of the unknown, disorientation, a future of uncertainty, and replaces it with the assurance that God is in control and that there truly is nothing to worry about.

1 Corinthians 4:15 NASB

"For all things are for your sakes, so that the grace which is spreading to more and more people may cause the giving of thanks to abound to the glory of God."

1 Corinthians 4:15 MSG

"Every detail works to your advantage and to God's glory: more and more grace, more and more people, more and more praise!"

Notice how similar 1 Corinthians 4:15 is to Romans 8:28. Compare these versions with the NIV and others to see that 1 Corinthians 4:15 emphasizes the spirit of gratitude through thanksgiving. God is glorified through our constant attitude of praise and gratitude that we give to him. Self help teaches us to have an attitude of gratitude; Romans 8:28 teaches us why we have this attitude. All of this is only a rung on the ladder of success that we all have to climb. Let us read about that next.

Chapter Five

Climbing the Ladder

Regardless of our own personal religious beliefs, we all want to advance as individuals as far as possible. This is what self help is all about. Each one of us has our own ladder to climb. No one else can climb it for you. This is not a competitive race. There is no competition. The very idea of competition is a false paradigm. In competition there is always a loser. In competition there are not enough trophies or prizes for everyone, therefore the concept of lack is introduced. In competition everyone else is your opponent, enemy, or against you in some way. God did not create a competitive universe. We actually live in a universe where everyone else wants to be our friend, and has an earnest desire to see us succeed. We live in a universe where we are surrounded by love, joy, and peace. Some people have chosen the dark path instead of the universe of love and peace. What universe they live in and what path they take is their choice. I prefer not to associate with such individuals. What universe you live in is your business, and your choice. It is all about perception. The people who go to heaven are there by choice. I can choose what thoughts I think; therefore I can choose my destiny. The knowledge of self improvement has never been more assessable to the public than now. This is no accident. God has planned this for a reason. If there was any time in history where humans needed personal improvement, it would be the last generation on earth. We need to help ourselves, and we need to help others help themselves. God is always there for us as a source of strength and guidance through the worst of times. In the book "Secret of the Ages": Volume Six, under the section titled What Do You Lack, Robert Collier says that "The purpose of existence is growth". One common example given in self-help books of this is trees. Trees are always growing. As soon as a tree stops growing it starts to die. I believe people are the same way. We need to always advance as an individual in some way or another.

Part of climbing the ladder of life is letting go. Jeremiah 29:13 in the New International Version says that "You will seek me and find me when you seek me with all your heart." Figuratively this is grabbing God with both hands. We cannot do this when we are holding on to something else. We have to let go. We have to let go of anything that has caused us pain, worry, anxiety, anger or resentment. Often the items of worldly prosperity have elements of stress attached to them. Climbing the ladder of life involves acknowledging God as the owner of all that we have, are, or ever will be. In this mindset we cannot be stressed out because with the absence of ownership comes the absence of the concept of loss. We cannot lose something we never had to begin with. With this mindset letting go comes easy and natural, and any type of stress just drifts away.

Chapter Six

Prosperity and Poverty

When I say the words "prosperity gospel", what images come to mind? Did God really promise us a rose garden? From what we just read in chapter one on 2 Timothy 3:12 it sounds more like we are promised a thorn bush. I like prosperity. Most normal people do, but prosperity has been one of Satan's most effective tools.

Matthew 19:21-24 AMP

"21Jesus answered him, If you would be perfect [that is, have that spiritual maturity which accompanies self-sacrificing character], go and sell what you have and give to the poor, and you will have riches in heaven; and come, be My disciple [side with My party and follow Me]. 22But when the young man heard this, he went away sad (grieved and in much distress), for he had great possessions. 23And Jesus said to His disciples, Truly I say to you, **it will be difficult for a rich man to get into the kingdom of heaven**. 24Again I tell you, **it is easier for a camel to go through the eye of a needle than for a rich man to go into the kingdom of heaven**."

It is not a sin to be wealthy, but throughout history every god following nation or group has strayed from gods will after being subjected to abundant prosperity for several generations. Before I continue any further I need to address the issue of the wealth of Jesus and his apostles. Some evangelists preach that Jesus and the apostles were wealthy. Then they preach that if your not wealthy like Jesus then it is the result if some secret sin or disobedience to the will of God. What a coincidence, Jobs friends said the same thing to Job. Note that God was so offended by what Job's friends had said that they were not even permitted to offer a prayer to god, Job had to do that on their behalf.

Luke 2:22-24 NKJV

"Now when the days of her purification according to the law of Moses were completed, they brought Him to Jerusalem to present *Him* to the Lord 23 (as it is written in the law of the Lord, *"Every male who opens the womb shall be called holy to the LORD"*), 24 and to offer a sacrifice according to what is said in the law of the Lord, *"A pair of turtledoves or two young pigeons."*

According to Leviticus chapter twelve Mary was supposed to bring a lamb for an offering. The reason she brought two turtle doves instead was because of poverty. Jews living in poverty could not afford a lamb and therefore were instructed to offer a pair of pigeons or turtledoves instead.

Matthew 8:20 NIV

"Jesus replied, "Foxes have holes and birds of the air have nests, but the Son of Man has no place to lay his head.""

Jesus was a homeless person. He was totally living by faith (see Habakkuk 2:4). His poverty drove him to full dependence upon his heavenly father for all his temporal and material needs. The fact that God the father permitted his only son to live in such poverty proves that God's priorities may be different than what we hear preached from the pulpit of many churches. Could it be that character development and a close relationship with God are more esteemed by God than material wealth or even life itself? Job's first ten children were adults when they were killed by a falling house. Like us all they had plans and dreams of a prosperous life ahead of them. Apparently God's will for them wasn't the life of luxury so often touted by some television evangelist.

2 Corinthians 8:9 ESV

"For you know the grace of our Lord Jesus Christ, that though he was rich, yet for your sake he **became poor**, so that you by **his poverty** might become rich."

There is something about "his poverty" that makes me think that Jesus wasn't rich. I admit that as a tax collector Matthew probably wasn't hurting for money in the early years of his ministry. Luke was a doctor so he was better off than the rest, but their work in the ministry was run on faith and donations. Anyway you look at it; the apostles were not rich, even self-help author Robert Collier admits to that (see Secret of the Ages volume 6, the master mind).

Philippians 3:8 NKJV

"Yet indeed I also count all things loss for the excellence of the knowledge of Christ Jesus my Lord, for whom **I have suffered the loss of all things**, and count them as rubbish, that I may gain Christ"

Paul states that he suffered the loss of all things. Where did some people get the idea that the apostles were wealthy? I cannot stand up in front of people and say "God's will for you is to be rich". There are too many variables and other priorities in the will of God for me to say that. God's will for us is to prosper, except when it interferes with the great plan he has for us all. There are more important agendas in the universe than our worldly prosperity; still we are striving for more wealth. In volume one of this series I quoted scripture supporting God's will in favor of us having wealth. Now we will look deeper into the subject to get a more accurate view of God and his will for us.

A clear definition of prosperity must be understood. Unfortunately God's definition of prosperity and society's definition may be completely different. This is where the chapter on the seen and the unseen (see volume 1 of this series) may be helpful. God looks ahead eons of time to determine what is best for us. We may be looking ahead a few years or decades. People often equate prosperity with things seen; God often equates prosperity with things unseen. Throughout scripture God has demonstrated his ability to grant material prosperity to individuals or nations in a short period of time, but this was never the overwhelming theme of scripture. If God's main focus was to turn us all into billionaires then we would all be billionaires. I suspect the antediluvian world had wealth far beyond what we have today, yet only eight people went into the ark. I believe the material wealth of Noah and his family was below the world average at that time.

Who would you say was more prosperous: Noah and his family who lost most every thing they had in the flood or every one else who lost all including eternal life? We are familiar with what the Bible says in favor of prosperity and wealth, but there other scriptures that we need to consider. Wealth can be used for good or it can be used for evil. Prosperity is something we should be cautious about. Let us look now at some verses that most prosperity gospel preachers tend not to use.

Proverbs 16:8 NCV

"It is better to be poor and right than to be wealthy and dishonest."

Proverbs 22:7, 16 NASB

"7The rich rules over the poor, And the borrower becomes the lender's slave. 16He who oppresses the poor to make more for himself or who gives to the rich, will only come to poverty."

Proverbs 23:4-5 MSG

"**Don't wear yourself out trying to get rich**; restrain yourself! Riches disappear in the blink of an eye; wealth sprouts wings and flies off into the wild blue yonder."

Proverbs 28:6, 20, 22 ESV

"Better is a poor man who walks in his integrity than a rich man who is crooked in his ways. 20A faithful man will abound with blessings, but **whoever hastens to be rich will not go unpunished**. 22A stingy man hastens after wealth and does not know that poverty will come upon him."

The Bible has both positive and negative comments on the subject of money. Here are some of the more positive verses.

Ecclesiastes 7:1, 11-12 MSG

"A good reputation is better than a fat bank account. Your death date tells more than your birth date. 11-12 **Wisdom is better when it's paired with money**, especially if you get both while you're still living. Double protection: wisdom and wealth! Plus this bonus: Wisdom energizes its owner."

Ecclesiastes 10:19 MSG

"Laughter and bread go together, and wine gives sparkle to life— but **it's money that makes the world go around**."

Proverbs 8:20-21 NKJV

"I traverse the way of righteousness, in the midst of the paths of justice, 21 that **I may cause those who love me to inherit wealth**, **that I may fill their treasuries**."

I propose that wealth can be equally beneficial or detrimental to ones life. Money is neutral. It is neither good nor evil. Our attitude toward worldly wealth can be a deadly snare or a blessing to others. The constant obsession with acquiring more wealth is a lifestyle not endorsed by scripture. It can ruin your life and your soul. Christians have higher priorities in their lives than the gratification of greed. We need to be confident in the fact that everything we need on earth to accomplish the mission that God has given us to do will be provided. Money can either be a tool or a drug; the choice is ours to make. We ether control money or money controls us. Satan would not hesitate for a moment to use the abundance of, or lack of wealth to manipulate us. We are not without help in this or any other tool that can be used against us. Just before Cain killed Abel God had a conversation with Cain. This is what God said:

Genesis 4:6-7 NASB

"Then the LORD said to Cain, "Why are you angry? And why has your countenance fallen? 7"If you do well, will not your countenance be lifted up? And if you do not do well, sin is crouching at the door; and its desire is for you, **but you must master it**."

Notice that sin is spoken of as an entity capable of desire. The kind of desire a predator has for its prey. But God has given us the power to master it. We must be the master of our wealth and thoughts. We must be the type of person that does not change due to any amount of accumulation or deprivation of wealth.

Chapter Seven

The big bad wolf

We are all pawns on the chessboard of life. The opposing kings represent God and Satan. God and Satan have agreed to the rules of the game.

Once upon a time mother hen decided to have baby chicks. And she did. The big bad wolf came to mother hen in protest and said "This is not fair. You're keeping all the baby chicks to your self! I have a legal right to baby chicks the same as you." Mother hen agreed. A meeting was convened and an agreement was reached by both parties. Mother hen and the wolf agreed that ten feet was a fair safety distance. Any baby chick that wandered more than ten feet from mother hen belonged to the wolf. The wolf said "furthermore I want our agreement to be confidential. No baby chick is to know about the ten foot rule" So the hen and wolf agreed that no specific information were to be given to the chicks. This was done so the game would be fair to the wolf. Baby chicks were to be given only vague information like "Stay close to mother hen." or "You're only safe when you're close to mother hen." The wolf said "I want one more thing. I want all the corn that baby chicks can eat." Mother hen agreed to that too.

At first most chicks stayed close to mother hen. One chick in particular ventured out a few feet from mother hen to get some corn and then ran back to eat it's corn. The chick thought to itself "It wasn't that bad, nothing happened to me" The next day this particular baby chick ran out to get some more corn, but this time it was more comfortable leaving the protection of mother hen. Some of the chicks wandered too far from mother hen and were eaten by the wolf. Other chicks wandered too far from mother hen only to find much corn and a kinder, gentler wolf willing to make a deal. The wolf said "I know what you really want. You want more corn. I will give you all the corn you want if you would just stand here and convince other chicks to come on over to me. There is plenty of corn for everybody." In time many chicks felt at home working for the wolf even though some did get eaten every now and then. After all, mother hen and the big bad wolf were so tall that the chicks never really noticed. Chicks are built to look down, not up. All baby chicks see is corn; that is all they really think about. One day one of the chicks fell into some misfortune. The chick slipped off a ledge and fell onto its side. While laying there on its side the chick did something it had not done before. The chick looked up. The chick saw mother hen and thought to itself "Maybe there are more important things in life than corn. I shall investigate this further". After a lengthy investigation the chick discovered that all corn came from mother hen. Excited about the new discovery, the chick ran around telling all the other chicks in the area. Instead of acceptance the chick was met with disbelief and ridicule, so the baby chick continued on with investigating things up. After more investigation it was discovered that mother hen not only created the corn, she also created the big bad wolf! Why was this so? Upon even further investigation it was discovered that in the beginning, there was only mother hen. There was no corn and no wolf. The wolf and the corn were only temporary. While here, the big bad wolf and the corn serve a purpose. The whole purpose of the corn and the wolf seems to be to test baby chicks. Baby chicks that pass the test live forever. One time there was not any corn around mother hen, so the chicks had a choice to do without or cross the line of safety. This was a test to see who the chicks loved more, the corn or mother hen. Baby chicks don't have much information, just enough to legally make a decision.

Remember that mother hen has always been fair to the big bad wolf. She does this to show everyone that she is fair through and through. So what do we do? We look up and realize that corn is not all there is in the universe.